CONNECTIONS CHANGE EVERYTHING

*How Smart Leaders Connect
Through Better Conversations*

Kimberly Layne

INDIE BOOKS
INTERNATIONAL

ISBN-13: 978-1-947480-93-3
Library of Congress Control Number: 2020900240

Designed by Joni McPherson, mcphersongraphics.com

INDIE BOOKS INTERNATIONAL, INC
2424 VISTA WAY, SUITE 316
OCEANSIDE, CA 92054

www.indiebooksintl.com

This book is dedicated to my mom and dad. To my dad, who sacrificed and strived to ensure that the three of us kids had access to a great education, adventure in nature, saw limitless boundaries, and adopted a good work ethic. Without this foundation of encouragement and discipline, educational opportunities, and love, I would not be where I am today. Dad, I know you are proud. I am thankful for all your love and support. To my mom, who exemplifies the most limitless heart of giving, nurturing, and helping others feel loved. She is the most amazing, gorgeous, selfless woman who ever walked on this planet, and who has modeled for me the nurturing power of unconditional love; of cooking, baking, and entertaining others with good food, conversation, and company. These qualities were also passed down by my mom's mom: Grandma, and my dad's mom: Nanna. These three were beautiful, amazing, strong, and loving women who are all ahead of their time. I hope that I too can leave a memorable and impactful legacy behind.

Contents

Preface. vii

1 Broken Off. 1

2 The Consequences Of Disconnection. 11

3 The Power Of Digital Technology 23

4 What Did You Say? (I Thought I Was Listening) 37

5 Difficult Conversations And Conflict Resolution 49

6 The Lost Meal: The Hidden Power Of Breaking Bread. . 63

7 A Corrected Connected Course. 79

Appendix

A The KCC Connection Corrections 93

B A Brief History Of Leadership 97

C About The Author 121

D Bibliography 123

E Acknowledgments 129

Preface

It was March 16, 2019, a beautiful sunny day coming after an unusually gloomy winter and spring in Newport Beach, California. I had been aching for sunshine. As I was standing at a Chevron station pumping gas on Bristol Street, I noticed that every single person around me was not enjoying the moment of this beautiful day. There were twelve other people not breathing in the fresh air, or holding their face up to the sun, or simply pausing for a moment while they pumped gas. *Everyone* was face to phone.

The five individuals at their corresponding pumps, the three people walking down the sidewalk, and the four customers in the Chevron mart were all glued to their devices. You would think an important news alert was just released, or in reality, probably a new client email or text.

Unbelievable, no one even realized anyone around them existed. They were self-absorbed with their phones, and oblivious to this gorgeous sunny day. *What a blissful moment lost for all of them*, I thought, and a foreshadowing of the future of the human existence.

We are slowly disengaging, pulling ourselves away from each other, denying ourselves the ability to be present and to truly be experiencing what is around us with all five senses. Probably, the more horrifying part to me is that I know for many people this is not intentional. It is just the effect of believing through advertising, that the eight-ounce piece of technology in your hand has the power to provide you with true joy, and human connection.

Why did I write this book? There are two reasons. The first one is the perception that digital technology provides us the connection we need, and the second impetus is to provide a platform for me to share my story and to lead by example in doing so. It is a story that is told repeatedly, with various versions and outcomes; some are resolved, some are hauntingly not.

I now publish this book as an adult who has found her healing, well-being, and true joy, and who has had the fortune of a successful and lengthy career in corporate America. As a mentor, consultant, and leader, I draw from my past journey, challenges, and success to help others who desire to grow and learn, and who are passionate about finding their true joy, connection, and purpose.

Through the Kimberly Connection Company, I bridge the gap between employers and their employees by educating and coaching leaders on how to have real conversations and build connection with their teams. Feeling and being more connected at work is a key component to an individual's happiness. It is proven that a joyful employee is a more productive, creative, and committed employee, and an asset to a company's bottom line.

With a strong formal education including a BBA, MBA, and a pursuit of a PhD in psychology, all bolstered by my extensive self-help reading, self-education, and corporate sales success, I am acutely aware of others in difficult positions.

You may be experiencing a gap, finding yourself just going through the motions, or only focusing on material outcomes. You may sit in your executive office comfortably, but when you walk the floors of your organization, you really don't know the individuals that occupy those seats. If you are always pushing your own agenda, half-listening to the people around you, and missing a basic human need of connection within your organization, then this book is for you.

Disconnection is just as much an indicator of life expectancy as is blood pressure and weight. Disconnection, in any area of our life, leads to a lack of joy, happiness, and peace. When it happens at work, where we spend so much of our time, it has a great impact on both our professional and our personal life. For you, the employer, your unhappy employees lead to a lack of engagement, productivity, and decreased profitability—a strong impact to your bottom line. I want to see our work environments become a place of supported growth, community, and fulfillment for both employees and employers.

We as humans can't survive on detachment, disassociation, and disconnection.

After reading this book, at *minimum*, you will have an increased awareness of your day-to-day interactions, and the opportunities you are missing for connection. Beyond that, you will likely take those daily interactions and create greater connection in your business life for success. You will come to know your employees as people, and you will treat them as such. At the highest level, you will realize that all of your interactions, professionally and personally, have an opportunity to be meaningful connections. You will choose to turn your daily interactions with clients and colleagues, and family and friends into meaningful genuine experiences that bring joy, fulfillment, and success.

I believe there are three areas that prevent people from interacting or connecting with others: (1) lack of transparency, (2) the overuse/dependence on technology, and (3) not really listening. Or what I like to say: The three things that lead to us feeling broken off, which I address in the first chapter.

Kimberly Layne
Newport Beach, CA
September 2019

Broken Off

"Everyone has a chapter they don't
want to read out loud."

—*Ellen DeGeneres*

This is a guidebook for leaders who are on a journey of
reflection. If you are willing to take this guided tour, you
should meet your tour guide. I want to share a personal
chapter from my life as we begin.

What is your chapter? I believe everyone at one point in their
life has had a secret they want to keep hidden. Maybe you are
still hiding yours.

Maybe it is a secret. Maybe it is a lie. Maybe it is an insecurity.
Maybe it is an addiction. We all have one. Big or small, it
is something that you are protecting and holding back, and
there is a lack of transparency. Transparency is the act of not
totally embracing or revealing our past, our present, and the
truth of what we believe in and who we really are.

By hiding something, we are not truly showing up with 100 percent of ourselves. We are burying or holding back a part of ourselves that we do not wish to share or expose to the rest of the world. This takes a vast amount of mental and emotional energy to (1) keep it buried and hidden from others, and (2) to try to not think about it. The immense effort in keeping a secret buried has an impact on productivity. Additionally, because we are consciously burying a part of ourselves, we are not fully engaging with all of ourselves. When we are only interacting with a portion of ourselves, that good side of ourselves we only want to present to the world, we are not truly allowing for real connection.

Not fully showing up and being transparent means we are half engaged in what we are doing. In our meetings, we are not as creative; we don't take risks in sharing new ideas. In our relationships, we are half-presenting ourselves, holding a vulnerable or insecure, shameful side of ourselves back, and we are not fully being present.

Hiding Secrets

Let's start with the big stuff. What's my chapter that I don't want to read out loud? My chapter begins with, "I was part of the statistic of being one out of three girls." Yes, one out of three girls that are sexually molested/abused at one point in their life. At the innocent, young age of ten, I was sexually molested by someone I and our family trusted. It rocked my world. I went from a happy, joyful, lighthearted, playful little girl full of sunshine, ponytails, and laughter to a shameful, confused, guilt-ridden, withdrawn human being. Worse yet, because of the threats of my abuser, and because he was someone our family trusted and respected, I felt I could not share the destructive molesting behavior with my family.

I was isolated, fearful, and disconnected. I now had a secret. A secret that I felt dirty and shameful about. I protected my sexual abuser, and then later in life, in my first marriage, my physically abusive husband. Out of fear of my life, and out of shame, guilt, and embarrassment, I hid that part of my life from everyone, *everyone*, including my loving family. It took a great deal of energy to keep that secret buried, and there is a consequence to hiding secrets. What the mind won't release and reveal, the body will suffer.

As a result of keeping my secret and protecting my sexual abuser, coupled with a desire to control my environment, I decided to control my body. At ten-years-old, I was on a crash course of dieting and low self-esteem. I went from 5' 9" and 136 pounds in the summer before fifth grade to ninety pounds by the start of sixth grade (less than eighteen months). I had a full-blown eating disorder that consumed me mentally and physically.

I remember being so weak from hunger that I would take all my energy and strength to pull my frail skeletal body up the stairs. I could only get up the stairs by swallowing the entire handrail with both arms and dragging myself slowly and painfully from stair to stair till I reached the top breathless and exhausted. Counting calories and exercise routines were the daily, minute, and second obsessions that kept me from having to think about the abuse. I used to be that fun, cute, healthy, confident, and happy little girl with lots of friends, full of great spirit, talkative, and attracting new friends wherever I went. Now I was broken off.

Beware Of Being Broken Off

At twelve, I was now a sullen, scary, emaciated, insecure, and fearful little girl who was the target of jokes, finger-pointing, and isolation. I was not only broken inside, but I was broken off.

For me, *broken off* means being disconnected, as if something has come between you and the world. Imagine a bridge that has then been cut in two by some circumstance, and you grasp the metaphor.

When we hold back secrets, lies, and are not transparent about who we are, we are only partially connecting with people by not showing up with all of who we are. We are broken off and cheating ourselves of true connection.

In September of 1976, I hit the bottom of this journey. I had collapsed at school, out of dehydration and exhaustion, and woke up lying frail and listless in a hospital bed hooked up to every IV, nutritional supplement, and hydration infusion you can imagine. My 5'9" frame was now down to eighty-four pounds of bones.

I remember my mom and dad visiting me in the hospital room, feeling helpless, frustrated, and desperate in trying to reach me, to help me, to connect with me. My dad approached me, tears in his eyes, gripped my wasted frame, and shook my feeble body and said, "Kimberly, you aren't going to make it out of here alive, unless you start eating. *You are going to die*."

In that very moment, I realized, "I don't want to die. I want to live. I don't want to starve myself to death. I have to figure this out."

So, from that day forward, I did begin to eat. But because I had still refused to share my secret with my family and was still protecting my abuser, I remained aloof. I was disconnected, and purposefully isolated myself from my family by going to my room after dinner to study. On weekends, I would spend hours in the kitchen baking while the family watched sports or television shows and choosing my own company over the company of others. Being around others created a need to exert an enormous amount of effort and energy to keep my secret from reaching the surface and to pretend that everything was okay.

I did not really have a close relationship with my mom, dad, or my two brothers, and existed superficially in going through the motions since the beginning of the sexual molestation. When interacting with friends, colleagues, and clients, I remember feeling half-present, as if I was always observing myself interacting with them, not really feeling like I was truly a part of the conversation. When everyone laughed wholeheartedly, I chuckled from my chest as opposed to a deep diaphragm of a belly laugh. I never would allow anyone in, to get too close, to share any vulnerability.

As I got older, this lack of truly connecting, of feeling happy and embracing myself, of not truly laughing—honestly laughing—and of feeling clean from my head to my toe, bothered me. I wanted that; I wanted to get back to the happy, joyous part of myself I lost twenty-four years ago.

Enter My Counselor

So, in June of 1999, I met with my counselor. She suggested that if I truly want to be free, I had to confront my abuser. Knowing how difficult and painful this would be, I was willing to put my fear and pain aside, in order to truly live life once again.

I remember when I called my molester, he answered the phone, stating, "I have been waiting for your call." Ugh! My stomach dropped. My palms began to sweat. I sucked in my breath. From that day forward, my healing and my return to joy began. He came out to Kansas City, where I was living, and met with me and my counselor.

Why did he agree? As he was still so close to our family, he saw my continued struggle and my abusive marriages. Secondly, he was holding on to that secret too. He also had much guilt. I think he agreed to go to help his guilt and to help me to move forward. He said he was sorry. I allowed for forgiveness (without forgetting), so that I could move on. He was not a serial molester.

Then, one by one, separately, I had each one of my family members—my mom, my dad, my older brother, and my younger brother—come to Kansas City and have a joint session with my counselor. These sessions, combined with the nurturing, healing, and supportive response that I received from my family, noticeably changed my aura and my energy. At the culmination of this emotional process, I began to feel the light.

It was evident that others did too. I had a wonderful and successful career as a medical device representative for Boston Scientific. I had numerous key hospitals where I spent a day in the cath lab, building relationships and selling peripheral vascular disease treatment products. One hospital in particular, St. Luke's Hospital, was a key target hospital. I was well known, liked, and respected within the lab by my key physicians and by others that saw me as a regular visiting representative.

The Monday following the completion of my confronting therapy sessions with my sexual molester and family, I walked into the cath lab as usual. I was to spend the day scrubbing in one of my key physicians. A cardiologist I did not have a strong professional relationship with touched me on the arm and stopped me. He said, "You seem different, like this weight has been lifted from you. I can't explain it. It is like you are freer, happier. You have a different energy about you." I let out a gasp of delight, and a big smile filled my face.

It worked. My counselor was right. Holding in that secret, constantly burying my pain and shame, actually sucked a part of myself in, depleted my joyous energy, and prevented me from fully showing up and sharing myself with the rest of the world. I now was present with all of myself, and this physician could feel that. I was now on the path to a connection correction in all of my relationships. *I was elated.*

What Is Your Chapter?

What are you holding on to? What is preventing you from truly showing up with all of yourself? More importantly, what is the consequence to your body (what the mind refuses to share, the body will reveal) to your relationships, to your connections, and to your happiness? It took me twenty-four years to reveal my secret. I was burying the ugly part of myself, the shameful part of myself, and only showing up with what I felt was appropriate and acceptable, and liked and safe to others.

For you, it may not be sexual abuse or physical abuse. It may be an addiction. It may be depression, overeating, a medical condition, or an insecurity. It could even be a lie. A lie that is keeping a part of you broken off. Whatever it is, share it and release it to someone. Don't let your secret continue to cut you off from the joy and connection you deserve.

I am not saying that we need to confess our addictions, victimizations, wrongs, abuse, or medical diagnosis to everyone at work, but we do need to talk to someone who cares about us—a friend, a counselor, a partner, a spiritual group, or a medical professional. When we share what we are hiding, we will grow acceptance of that part of ourselves. We will fully embrace that part of ourselves, and now be able to fully show up in our lives, at work, at home, and in our relationships. Once I allowed that side of myself to be revealed, I and others began accepting the entire me.

When I began loving all of myself, my relationships, my connections, and my joy changed. *I was no longer broken off.*

Now let's continue our journey of leadership reflection.

Connection Correction #1

What secret are you hiding? What story are you not telling? What lie are you holding on to? Nathaniel Branden said: "When we bury our feelings, we also bury ourselves. It means we exist in a state of alienation. We rarely know it, but we are lonely for ourselves." By not revealing what you are burying, hiding, or lying about, you are not fully being present. Therefore, you are not showing up with all of you and the best version of yourself, as a leader. Your vulnerability is the best, most relatable part of yourself. Find a friend, colleague, medical professional, or a spiritual or religious advisor you trust to reveal, to embrace, and to accept this part of yourself and be on your way.

Chapter 2

The Consequence Of Disconnection

"The need for connection makes the consequences of disconnection that much more real and dangerous."

—Brené Brown

What happens when someone is disconnected? The need for connection and community is a basic developmental human need throughout our lives. Without it, we are withdrawn, depressed, and anxiety-provoked. For some, the suffering can be so unbearable that the emptiness may even lead to suicide.

In a *Psychology Today* article, written by Robert Weiss LCSW, CSAT-S, who is Senior Vice President of the National Clinical Development for Health, titled "The Opposite of Addiction is Connection," and agreed upon and expressed in the TED Talk titled "Everything You Think You Know

About Addiction is Wrong," by British journalist Johann Harir, said their available research states that the opposite of addiction is not sobriety, but connection. In this article, it states that addiction is not about the pleasurable effects of the substances abused, but it is the user's inability to connect in healthy ways with other human beings that cause them to choose the addicted substance.

The article continues to state that ten percent of people who try an addictive substance actually become addicts. Over time, a person's initial experience of pleasure is not what leads them back to that addictive substance again and again, to his or her detriment.

I am not a big fan of rats, and I would guess you are not either. However, rats appear to have the greatest similarity to humans as social creatures in many of the same ways. They need stimulation, company, play, drama, sex, and interaction to stay happy. In addition, we humans need to be able to trust each other and to also feel emotionally connected. Given this similarity, Canadian psychologist Bruce Alexander performed an experiment with rats. He placed the rats in empty cages, alone, with two water bottles: one with pure water, the other with heroin-infused water (Alexander, *The Globalization of Addiction*). As expected, as time passed, the rats would uniformly get hooked on and eventually overdose from heroin. So, the initial conclusion by researchers was that the potential of extreme pleasure, in and of itself, is addictive.

Alexander chose not to believe this and continued the experiment. He guessed that the rats went to the heroin because the cages were so small and there were no other stimuli, other than the heroin. Wouldn't we all get high out of sheer boredom? He then created an experiment called "the rat park," and utilized a cage approximately two hundred times larger than the typical isolation cage. The cage contained hamster wheels and multi-colored balls to play with, plenty of tasty food to eat, and spaces for mating and having little rat babies. He decided to put not just one rat in each cage, but twenty rats in each cage, both male and female. Once this lovely environment was created, he then introduced the heroin by offering one bottle of pure water and one bottle of heroin water. Fascinatingly, the rats refused and ignored the heroin, and preferred connecting with the other rats through mingling, playing, mating, and eating. To add to these different results, he reintroduced the original rats that became hooked on the heroin out of isolation and boredom to this rat pack, and they too chose social stimulation and connection over heroin.

Social adjustment studies done in the early 1950s, by John Bowlby and other researchers, analyzed the reactions of small children when they were separated from their parents (Howe, *Attachment Across Life Course*). It was concluded that having a strong essence of a safe, trusting, and reliable caregiver as an infant, toddler, and a young child is a direct relationship to one's ability to be happy and well-adjusted and feel overall emotionally healthy into adult life. This leads to connecting and trusting others while building healthy relationships. Children denied that intimacy, connection, and a safe environment early in life tend to struggle with trust and connection later in their adult life. As Alexander stated, "securely attached individuals tend to feel comfortable in and to enjoy the human rat park, while insecurely attached people typically struggle to fit in and connect."

As Weiss continues to explain, "The good news is that people with insecure attachment styles are not locked into this approach for life. With proper guidance and a fair amount of conscious effort the individuals who were not graced with secure attachment in childhood (and therefore the ability to easily connect in adulthood) can learn to securely attach. By seeking help through therapy, support groups, and various other healthy and healing relationships individuals can create over time what is known as 'earned security.'" And in my opinion, a corrected connection. They are no longer broken off and isolated.

How Does Disconnection Translate Into The Work Environment?

Disconnection affects employee engagement. Employee engagement is a property of the relationship between an organization and its employees. An engaged employee is one who is fully absorbed by and enthusiastic about their work and so takes positive action to further the organization's reputation and interests.

Feeling connected at work includes two things: (1) feeling safe enough to be transparent, open, and vulnerable, and (2) working in a culture that supports and creates a feeling of connection so that we feel a part of something, have a common purpose, and our presence counts as employees and as human beings. Feeling connected versus just interacting in our work environment improves employee engagement, which improves quality, effort, productivity, and employee retention. It also equals "joy," which is proven to directly correlate to greater employee engagement, and involvement and pride in the work one is performing.

When an employee is happy, there is increased participation, productivity, and quality, coupled with a feeling of safety within the culture to express and take risks on ideas with an increased feeling of loyalty to their organization. Russell Ackoff, a renowned organizational thinking expert, states, "If there is not joy in work, you won't get productivity, and you won't get quality! Joy is increased productivity." Not fully engaging, not feeling or being connected costs the US economy roughly $350 billion a year, according to McLean and Company (Warner 2018). Not being connected translates into lost productivity, poor engagement, reduced quality, and significant employee attrition.

The Corporate Leadership Council (Warner 2018), which studied the engagement level of 50,000 employees around the world, reported two important findings:

- Engaged companies grow profits as much as *three times faster* than their competitors.

- Highly engaged employees are *eighty-seven percent less likely* to leave the organization.

Gallup conducts a study annually of over 50,000 businesses that employ almost one and a half million employees over thirty-four countries, in order to evaluate the effect of employee engagement on a business' success. Repeatedly and consistently, work organizations that score in the top half of employee engagement have double the odds of success versus those in the bottom half. Additionally, for those companies and corporations that rank in the 99th percentile of engagement they demonstrate *four* times the success rate. Gallup attributes the success of these high-ranking organizations to the relationship between high employee engagement and nine key performance outcomes:

- 37 percent lower absenteeism
- 25 percent lower turnover (in high-turnover organizations)
- 65 percent lower turnover (in low-turnover organizations)
- 28 percent less shrinkage
- 48 percent fewer safety incidents
- 41 percent fewer patient safety incidents
- 41 percent fewer quality incidents (defects)
- 10 percent higher customer metrics
- 21 percent higher productivity
- 22 percent higher profitability

Interestingly, according to PayScale, successful Fortune 500 high-tech companies like Amazon and Google have some of the highest turnover rates with median tenure to be one year and 1.1 year respectively, despite well-above-average median salaries. Granted, some of it can be attributed to the shortage and intense recruiting and poaching effort for high-end tech talent in the high-tech industry, but I believe much of it can be attributed to their limited focus on employee retention and engagement. These two organizations may be erring on the side of sourcing top talent (young), pay them well, and then create extraordinary expectations of performance and workload than creating a culture of development and long-term success for their people. Eventually the employee reaches a point where the robust and healthy remuneration stops outweighing the misery, exhaustion, and lack of work/life balance and they eventually leave.

Three key elements behind effective employee engagement do not include money. Yes, competitive salaries and compensation packages are necessary for baseline engagement, but it is the "sense of belonging," and "feeling a part of a community," that positively contributes to employee retention.

The father of employee engagement, William Kahn, a professor of organizational behavior at Boston University's Questrom School of Business, identified this need for community and belonging back in 1990, and broke it down into three key elements behind effective employee engagement. Employees need to feel:

- Purpose: that their work is meaningful and makes a difference;

- Valued: that they are valued as a person, trusted and respected; and

- Secure: that the culture they work in and the people they work with provide for a secure and safe place to express themselves which contributes to their self-confidence.

Community and belonging means connection. In order to feel connected, (1) one needs to be able to show some vulnerability, and to show up with all of themselves, and (2) the culture that is expressed within an organization needs to safely allow that vulnerability and openness with a strong element of trust.

Contrast the environment of high-tech companies to several of the California branches of a top American financial security company. This company, in some of its California offices, has recently adopted a different environmental layout that supports a more open and transparent corporate culture in order to reduce turnover and to increase employee engagement. They have moved from a hierarchical structure of formality, segregation typical of financial companies, to an open format of freedom, accessibility, and community.

Gone are the numerous high-backed cubicles that leave no visibility to the occupants they are hosting. No longer are there separation between executives and associates from one side of the building to the next inclusive of separate bathrooms, breakrooms, and lunchrooms. Now, executives and associates are blended on the same floor and can peer from open offices with no higher than shoulder enclosures. Additionally, there is no office assignment; office space, conference rooms, and focus rooms are accessed at choice, depending on the day's agenda. The visibility of heads over office walls allows for easy communication to ask questions and relay information with a human element versus texting or emailing. Additionally, there are ongoing mentorship programs for all aspiring associates that empowers individuals to ask questions, build a safe and trusted relationship, solve problems with someone who has more experience, and ask for guidance or insight in certain situations.

Connection Correction #2

What is missing in your corporate culture to drive employee retention and engagement? Interview your employees to find out if they feel valued and respected, that their work and their contributions make a difference, and they feel safe to take risks in thoughts, ideas, and in action. Is there a sense of belonging?

As leaders and as top executives, I believe we perceive vulnerability as weak. Instead, we need to consider it a strength. Sharing your dark side or reading your chapter out loud makes you vulnerable and open for judgment, criticism, and ridicule. However, as leaders, when we open up and share our vulnerability, we become more relatable, and therefore more effective leaders. It takes a huge amount of strength to "expose" yourself, because when doing so, you are saying you are strong enough to withstand the judgment, the criticism, and the ridicule in order to be authentic.

I remember a story about a well-known CEO who was perceived as a stand-offish, harsh, and demanding person because of his desire for perfection from his employees and the resulting criticism that ensued when an employee failed to deliver. There was a definite barrier between him as a leader and his employees, even those directly reporting to him. One day he revealed that he held this high standard for his employees because he had had that high standard held for himself by his father, always trying to win his father's approval, respect, and affection. When this leader shared this chapter of his life, his *story*, after his father had passed, he became more authentic, relatable, and approachable as a leader. His employees had new respect and understanding for him that translated into employees feeling more engaged. The culture began to change. He was a better leader by featuring his vulnerability.

Sometimes what we think we need to hide to be liked and respected, is the very thing we need to reveal to attain what we are looking for. For me, I always felt that I had to be perfect to be loved. But, in trying to be perfect and attempting to project that image to others, I was distancing myself from others, was sometimes perceived as unapproachable, and therefore I felt not loved, or not liked. Now, in revealing my chapter of vulnerability and imperfections, I am more relatable and more loved. It is a funny dynamic. I thought I had to be perfect to be loved. I now realize I am more loved being imperfect. What opposes exposes.

Connection Correction #3

As a leader or executive, what vulnerability, story, or relatable aspect of yourself can you share with your team and your employees that will make you less perfect and more liked? Try it out on your immediate team and see the results. Then try it out on a larger audience. When we risk being authentic, we gain connection, engagement, joy, and success.

Chapter 3

The Power Of Digital Technology

"A new survey out says 64 percent of Americans own a smartphone. Which is interesting because in a related survey, 100 percent of smartphones say they own an American."

—Jimmy Fallon

D o you know anyone who does not have a smartphone, above the age of ten and below the age of ninety? The adoption of digital technology continues to accelerate.

According to Statista statistics, smartphone subscription as a percentage of the US population went from 20.2 percent in 2010 to over 70 percent in 2018 with smartphone sales to reach over $80 billion in 2019 (Baron 2016).

Smartphones have connected individuals who might have in the past been isolated. They have allowed for connection of all of us to each other, with the simple dial of a number, instantly. It has allowed for the ability to see (Apple FaceTime or video applications like Zoom) or talk with loved ones, clients, or colleagues, no matter what time zone, country, or continent. One can argue that it has increased connectivity. The world is a smaller place and technology can connect us when we are distances apart. We can reach anyone anytime, and almost anywhere.

I can remember the first bag phone in my car. It was a clumpy thing that looked like a small vacuum cleaner that took up the entire center console of my car. Or dialing a pay phone in the lobby of one of my top targeted hospitals as a medical device representative in order to page a surgeon to convince them to meet with me to sell my peripheral vascular wires, stents, and balloons. It was not a role of quarters that I was carrying, but a credit card size AT&T Corporate Calling Card where you had to dial a minimum of twenty-five numbers: first the 1-800 access number, then your PIN, then the ten digit number in order to make a phone call. It took five minutes just to initially get connected.

Or how about the non-wireless house phones, which would only let you travel twelve feet or the length of the cord during your conversation, and certainly not outside? You had a house phone practically in every room. Now we have the ability to talk while we walk, and while we drive, indoors or outdoors. We can "reach out and touch someone," pretty much anywhere and at any time, provided we have cell coverage. Additionally, we don't necessarily even need to dial and to speak. Smartphones and the internet have allowed us to ping a colleague, client, or friend across the hall or across the nation, instantly with an email or a text. It's practically magic compared to thirty years ago.

The average age when a child receives a cell phone is ten. Any earlier than that and experts believe a child's brain does not naturally, and with effort, seek out its own dopamine fix, and instead will resort to the easiest fix, which is an iPad or phone screen. Additionally, because of that feel-good feeling that comes with interacting with technology, it can disconnect our kids from their basic needs of sleep, nutrition, fresh air, and physical activity. My bigger concern is that this technology will also disconnect them from their higher human and developmental need of having a sense of belonging, feeling connected, and finding some meaning and value to their life. Instead of sharing and communicating at the dinner table, playing hopscotch or skateboarding outside, or choosing a team sport to play in, our kids may be looking at an iPad or smartphone. Unfortunately, as we get older, we are still gravitating toward the screen for an easy, quick, feel good, dopamine rush of a text, Instagram feed, Facebook feed, or work email.

How many of you remember summer block parties? When the end of your street was blocked off, and all your neighbors showed up with homemade potato salad, baked beans, brownies, and grills fired up with the smell of hot dogs and hamburgers. Music would loudly boom from someone's big boombox, while all the neighborhood kids would be running around playing a game of tag. Adults socialized while drinking their favorite adult beverage and laughing and joking as they reconnected over shared stories. I can't remember the last time I was at a block party. Can you? I imagine today, and I laugh at the thought, that block parties of today are more like a block webinar. Whereby each of us is sitting in our own chair, at the table, in our own house, with face to a laptop or iPad screen, and earphones plugged in to our favorite station. We attempt to interact with our neighbors through some video application, and our plate sits, filled with store-bought potato salad and a microwaved hot dog. What do you feel would be missing?

I am just as guilty of being enticed by the sound of a new email when it arrives, or the ping of a text, as you are. As our days are so hectic, we keep trying to squeeze more in our days with the same twenty-four hours we always had. Our workloads are so large that we, oftentimes, in order to finish a task or to get an answer, blurt out a text or craft an email to a friend, client, or colleague instead of picking up the phone, scheduling a lunch meeting, or walking down the hall to someone's office. We feel that *we don't have the time* for that personal interaction, and sometimes we just don't want to be involved or bothered.

But in reality, we actually get more and can even learn more when we sometimes choose to forsake technology and put in effort to connect face-to-face, or at least via the phone. I find it sad that in today's world, face-to-face and voice-to-voice are secondary to digital communication. A friend of mine has a twelve-year-old daughter who says that none of her friends call her, they just text her, and she loves the fact her dad always calls her on the phone. He is the only one. A 2018

Oxford Economics reported study confirms, unsurprisingly, that digital connections are much more common across the nation than personal interactions. It states that adults are almost twice as likely to interact "several times a week or more" with friends and family they don't live with via text or instant message than by meeting up with them in person, or calling them on the phone (*Oxford Economics*, "The Sainsbury Living Well Index," May 2018).

Going back to my block party comments, this same study mentions that baby boomers, working or not, scored slightly higher than average on social connection indicators. This higher-than-average score is because they have more neighbor interactions and probably remember and have experienced a block party, or at minimum, know their neighbors' names and converse with them on a regular basis in person. They state that around one in five baby boomers chat to their neighbors most of the time, compared to less than one in ten adults from younger generations.

I am concerned about how I see technology easily and unconsciously driving us apart. Under the guise of efficiency, expedience, and productivity, digital technology has allowed us to communicate differently and extensively, no doubt with FaceTime, video chat, texting, and emailing, but I believe technology also isolates and blocks us from having a true connection. We are slowly destroying our humanity and removing all human touch points, electively, by choosing digital interactions first.

Instead of walking down the hall to talk to a colleague, we send them a text; instead of having a ten-minute conversation/meeting, we send them an email. Instead of meeting colleagues or clients in person or over lunch, we conduct a Webex video conference. For many of us that work from home, virtual applications like Zoom and Skype make it easy for us to conduct business with clients and colleagues. Additionally, retailers like Amazon, Walmart, Chewy, and Target, just to name a few, make it a one-click wonder to order and have pretty much anything delivered, from dog toys to toiletries, within twenty-four hours to our doorstep. And, between meal-making services like Blue Apron, nearby grocery store chains, and mobile meal-deliver apps like Grubhub and DoorDash, we can have a plethora of dining and meal preparation options, such that we will never starve.

As a single woman living alone and working from home, I could literally exist in a solitary, isolated environment for days using the above stated resources. I could easily remove all true human touch points. However, I find when I have spent a day or two without much real social interaction, in order to complete a book, edit my inspirational speaking content, or a busy virtual day with consulting clients, I crave social interaction. I have an aching desire to get out and connect in person, with friends or family, or at minimum, if no one is available, take myself out to dinner in order to have some connection and conversation with the person sitting next to me.

The 2018 *Oxford Economics* study referred to earlier states that the frequency with which we meet, speak, and meaningfully connect with friends and family, neighbors, and others is shown to have a positive association with our well-being and joy. Boy, do I feel this and live this every day. In contrast, they stated that there was no association, neither positive nor negative, between someone's well-being and interacting digitally with email, text messaging, or social media consumption, all else being equal. Their basic analysis states: *Real social connections* are essential to living well, and that digital interactions are no substitute.

How many of you have had the joy and pleasure of online dating? I have, and because of the many hilarious and unfortunate experiences, it quite possibly could be the subject of my next book. I find it extremely funny that online dating consists of writing a profile about yourself, including your hobbies, dislikes, must-haves for your future partner, your best physical attributes, and at minimum, at least three of the most attractive photos of yourself, preferably one in full length and of course no sunglasses. Then the online search begins with picture or profile likes, online messaging, and swiping right for like and left for dislike. It is all done two-dimensionally with visual and written clues that identify someone as attractive enough to be a potential date. What are we all seeking in this process? Are we all seeking love, attraction, and chemistry? Chemistry is the very substance of that dopamine of attraction.

What is missing on a two-dimensional dating site? It's that aura and intangible energy we can't predict or define, called chemistry. Hysterical! And, that chemistry can only be felt, truly be sensed, and defined to be a possible attraction, when we finally get the chance to meet our potential match in person. That same element of energy and aura of face-to-face communication is why meeting and talking in person is so critical and adds so much value and meaning to our life. It is the energy that connects us and provides us with a sense of belonging and community. Needless to say, online dating has not been successful for me, despite knowing that many have been able to find their dream catch.

My fear is we are relying on digital technology in work and in our life too heavily and we are allowing it to replace efforts to create true connection with people in all areas of our life. If we choose to replace people with technology and rely less and less on our true human connections, we are setting ourselves and our kids up for severe depression, isolation, and being broken off.

From 1986 to the year 2000, the CDC states that the suicide rate declined steadily. In sharp contrast, from the year 2000 to 2014, the suicide rate in the United States rose 24 percent and is approaching a thirty-year high. What else do you think was going on around the year 2000? The World Wide Web as we know it started around 1992 and was quite robust by the year 2000, and from the year 2000 to 2014, mobile phone subscriptions exponentially increased to over five billion users throughout the world, and over three billion people access the internet on a regular basis. The Nokia phone, in 1996, was the first device with internet capabilities and the iPhone was first launched in June 2007. Psychological studies have suggested that there is a relationship between anxiety and the use of mobile devices, coupled with their ability to steal our attention away from true human connection (Shoukat 2019). Cell phones and digital technology create more separateness and isolation between us and our family and friends and provide us with a temporary false dopamine fix. I am not surprised at this coincidental rise in suicide rates.

Just as calculators have destroyed the need to be able to do math, I am concerned the next generation won't be able to write a complete, correct, and meaningful sentence unless of course they incorporate five emojis and eighteen abbreviations. I am concerned that the art of customer service will resort to swiping left or swiping right.

Think about it: as mentioned in my isolation of being single and ability to work from home, we really don't have to communicate and connect with anyone; we can simply interact. We can avoid truly seeing, hearing, or feeling people as we never have to hear, see, or feel their facial expressions, their joy or disappointment, their anger or their elation. We can send a text, not respond to a text, send an email, delete the email, not have a conversation, delay a response, like, unlike, send an emoji, unfriend, friend, or swipe left, all at the expense of human connection and in an effort to disconnect.

Or, what about the art of ghosting? Can you imagine in the middle of a face-to-face conversation with someone, you just get up and leave with no closure, "excuse me," or goodbye? It would be considered quite disrespectful and downright rude. However, in the exchange of texting, it is quite common and acceptable. Really?

What happened to the art of breaking up with someone in person? Can you believe I have been broken up with over voicemail? And the last one was the worst—it was done over a text. This is someone that I dated for over six months. Face-to-face communication can be difficult, but having an in-person conversation with someone is also showing up with true vulnerability, authenticity, and respect for the human experience. It is important for our humanity to feel and to connect, and to see the implication of our words or actions on other people versus allowing ourselves to disconnect from the emotion and go numb. We all have to get back to communicating in person verbally, not nonverbally, and to set up models of connected behavior for others or risk the threat of our offspring and future generations to grow up absent of any interpersonal skills.

Putting Digital Technology In Its Place

One of my favorite commercials for smartphones shows two men in suits at a conference table and one man gets up to leave to go to the bathroom. No sooner has the one man left the room when the cell phone on the conference table, near the remaining man, begins to ring. He picks up the cell phone and answers the call. Cut to the phone whereby an attractive woman is seen doing a strip tease dance to music. A minute after this has played out, the one man who had left the room opens up the door to the conference room and returns. Immediately, the man in the conference room shuts down the phone and places it on the conference table, and quickly announces, "Your wife just called."

When and where is having your smartphone appropriate so that we leverage its value but ignore its temptation? Here are some of my suggestions from Kimberly's Connection Tips: Test them out by slowly adopting them once a week or month and gradually increase their frequency based on your success and others' receptivity.

Mobile-Free Meetings (MFM): Virgin America utilizes this technique in its meetings whereby any meeting invite that has a MFM designation is defined as a *mobile-free meeting*, which means that everyone leaves their phone(s) in their office, or deposits them into a basket at the entrance to the conference room. Everyone knows that for forty-five minutes, their full attention is focused on the conversation, and the meeting and agenda at hand for the highest level of contribution, collaboration, creativity, planning, productivity, and solutions. Everyone also knows that because the meeting is only forty-five minutes long, they will get the remaining fifteen minutes back of a typical sixty-minute meeting in order to interact with their phones to respond to emails, texts, etc. before they head back to their desk or their next meeting. Try to conduct at least one meeting a week as an MFM and see how your team reacts and how much gets accomplished. Progressively introduce more per month, where most appropriate.

Mobile-Free Meals: Like *mobile-free meetings*, there can be *mobile-free meals*. Leave the phones and the digital devices somewhere far enough away so you must get up and get it, or at minimum, turn it off, so that we are not tempted by the tune of an email, phone call, or text. I truly feel being present, listening, communicating, and enjoying a meal together is such a pleasure and one of the best experiences to create human connection. I am sure all of us have had the experience when meeting someone for lunch or dinner or having your kid at the table and on his or her smartphone, of not being connected, let alone feeling and being heard. Breaking bread together is such an ancient, communal experience that not only feeds our stomachs, it feeds our souls (more to come later in "The Lost Meal" Chapter 7). Try to incorporate this rule at *all* your meals with colleagues, clients, friends, and family. At home, you may need to start off with one meal a week and fill that silence with conversation starters around the table, such as, "If you wanted to plan a vacation, where would you go?" or, "Tell me one good thing that made you happy today." Even if there is some silence, eventually it will be filled with interesting conversation, personal insights, and you are starting on your way to improving your connections.

Talk and Touch: I call this the "KCC Three Points of Daily Connection." (KCC stands for The Kimberly Connection Company.) Find three separate moments throughout your day. It can be mid-morning, mid-afternoon, and at the end of your day. It can be on your drive to work, a moment to break up your workday, and on your drive home. Find what works best and change it up each day. For example, instead of texting a friend in the morning, you could pick up the phone. Instead of emailing a colleague on an issue, you could walk down to their office or set up a lunch meeting. Toward the end of your day, again, instead of texting someone, you could pick up the phone and call, or possibly even stop by. Try these easy connection options:

- Instead of sending a text, pick up the phone and call

- Instead of sending an email, get up out of your chair and walk down the hall

- Instead of having a phone conversation or virtual meeting, meet in person or schedule a lunch or dinner meeting

- Reach out personally via phone or in person to someone you don't necessarily have an agenda, excuse, or need to call

By doing so, you will naturally increase your human points of connection, and probably feel a bit more joyful. I am also willing to bet that you will see an improvement in your relationships and connection with that client, colleague, friend, neighbor, or family member over time, when you introduce these three points of connection a day. I challenge you to seeing the connection correction in your own life.

Now that we have you reaching out and connecting in person, or at minimum, over the phone, let's get you ensuring that connection in person is the most fulfilling for both (and all) of you, in the next chapter.

Connection Correction #4

Introduce mobile-free meetings at least once a week. Introduce mobile-free meals at least once a week at home, and in all business meals, where possible. Exercise three points of connection a day, where you opt to exercise your ability to create human connection versus using digital technology by calling, meeting in person, or sharing a meal.

Chapter 4

What Did You Say? (I Thought I Was Listening)

"Most people do not listen with the intent to understand; they listen with the intent to reply."

—Stephen R. Covey

How many times have you crossed paths with someone you know, and they ask: "How are you doing?" Then they keep on walking, never stopping to hear your answer. As a result, you stop in your tracks, cease talking, and possibly turn around and stare at their exiting back. You are left standing alone in space with your feelings and words hanging in the air.

In that situation, when someone is really not listening, it conveys that they do not care enough about you to even wait for your response to their questions. It leaves you with a disgruntled emptiness in the pit of your stomach and a bruised self-esteem. We are not quite sure why we even bothered to share our mood or feelings as they fell flat on the ears of the intended recipient.

Why should we ask questions if we sincerely don't care to listen or to hear the answer? We all want to be heard and acknowledged. If we feel we are not being listened to, it can be stressful, anxiety-provoking, and create feelings of low self-worth, as if we don't measure up to the non-listener.

If this is an environment in which you work and regularly communicate, it will cause you to be less creative, candid, and risky. At the extreme, if these feelings are constantly projected on ourselves, it can lead to unhappiness and depression. You will tend to withhold information, start to disconnect, be less engaged, and eventually choose to leave the company.

As a female surrounded by males in a successful corporate role, I remember it being difficult to find an opportunity to speak and be heard. Instead of taking this personally, and reflecting it inward, I chose to mention those thoughts to my superior. He was very supportive and knew that when I chose to speak it usually had significant value and brought a unique perspective. In future meetings, knowing the team could get quite loud, which made it difficult to interject, he would circle the room and ask if I or others had something to contribute.

Taking that initiative on my part and getting the response I did from my boss made me feel acknowledged and respected as an employee. As a result, the climate was more conducive to creativity and taking risks. It helped not only me but the entire team, as we created a culture and space for taking risks without judgment and to be heard.

I have chosen to highlight three typical listening personas that you may encounter:

The Self-Focused Interrupting Listener. Taking a step out of the work environment to my personal dating life, I remember dating a guy. Let's call him Jerry. Every time I or anyone shared a story, Jerry immediately would interrupt and share a bigger or better story about himself and his experiences. It would leave me and any other person talking feeling not heard, talked over, unimportant, and frustrated. It was annoying and obviously one of the reasons I no longer continued to date Jerry. It hit on my self-esteem by constantly being interrupted mid-sentence and never able to complete my thought or story, let alone feeling like what I was saying was not important. Listening only to be able to find a trigger to jump in and switch the conversation over to ourselves is really not "hearing" what someone is saying. Being constantly self-focused and interrupting is very self-centered, rude, and a sure way to maintain separation.

Don't be a Jerry!

The Personal Agenda At All Costs Listener. A similar version to the self-focused interrupter is the individual who only is listening for the sole purpose of directing the conversation to meet and accomplish his/her agenda. Obviously, in a sales conversation, we do try to keep boundaries on the conversation so that we gather the necessary information needed to determine if this is a viable sales opportunity. We ask questions to identify the key decision-makers, possible objections to the sale, executive buy-in and timelines for decision making, and negotiate the conversation to progress through the necessary stages to close the deal. With that being said, there is a fine line to balancing your needs as a salesperson and those of your potential client. In general, we need to err on the side of being present, listening, and willing to not "force" our agenda so that we form trust. At the end of the day, if you haven't formed a trusting relationship, there will be no sale, no matter how much information you are able to gather.

In my past life as a salesperson, I remember many times when I had set up a follow-up meeting with a prospect for the purpose of mutually progressing the sale, and realized at the onset of the meeting that it was clear that the initial agenda set for the meeting was not going to fly. I was sensitive that my prospect was preoccupied and was dealing with an important family matter or a recent corporate announcement. I chose to be present and to listen to my potential client rather than holding tight to my sales agenda.

Being sensitive to the energy and issue at hand created a huge amount of trust and respect between us. As a result, the next meeting with my client began with an apology for the interruption and a thank you for my sensitivity. Additionally, because of the trust and respect I created in being sensitive to their agenda, I was able to gather the necessary insight I needed for the sales process with more transparency than before.

In not forcing my agenda, my sensitivity to my clients as human beings and truly listening to them earned their trust and built a connection with them. Listening "without an agenda" means to stay present in the words being spoken, the vulnerability that is being exposed, and more importantly, the connection that is being created.

Keep in mind that *listening without an agenda* does not always mean that you don't have an agenda. It means that you are listening to hear, not listening to navigate the conversation. After the individual has completed their thought and you have gained full understanding by paraphrasing or asking clarifying questions, it can be your time to be listened to as well.

The Multitasker Listener. What someone has to say is an engaging process and should take your full attention. However, many of us think we can multitask or partially engage in something else and be effective listeners. It gets even more difficult to not multitask if you are listening to someone who has the gift of rambling, switching topics, and *failing to get to the point.*

As a result, the temptation strikes. We want so badly to check our phone, peek at our unopened emails, or glance at our watch. We are self-acclaimed experts at multitasking and responding to external technological stimuli, that the minute something is not keeping our attention, we want to feed and fill that space. How does that make you feel when someone is multitasking while you are speaking to them? Especially if you are sharing something emotional and or very important to you. Not good, right?

Resist that temptation and decide that you want to be present for this person. Close your laptop, turn your phone on silent or off, and take a deep breath. Look that individual in the eye and pay attention. Acknowledge them through active questioning or paraphrasing and leave them feeling validated and heard, not empty and invalidated.

To be listened to is a validating, warm, loving feeling. The opposite is demeaning, cold, and disempowering. Michael Nichols, in his book, *The Lost Art of Listening*, states that: "We never outgrow the need to have our feelings known. That is why a sympathetic ear is such a powerful force in human relationships and why the failure to be understood is so painful."

The Heart Of Listening

Nichols likes to call it the art of listening, while I choose to call it the *heart of listening*. If you are truly listening, you are hearing and feeling what the other person is saying with your heart; and the person being listened to can feel your interest and connection.

Before I get into the attributes of a good listener, let's define the difference between hearing and listening. Listening is more the act of making sense of what someone is saying, paying thoughtful attention, and trying to connect with them. Hearing has more to do with the physiological act of perceiving sound and the special sense by which noise and tones are received as stimuli. I feel like we have to actively engage ourselves and make a mental note to listen to someone when they begin to speak, as we so often have our own internal dialogue and agenda running through our head, that we just absorb the sounds and external stimuli.

We need to hear those sounds, interpret their meaning, and respond to the person such that it improves.

I believe there are three key components to listening with your heart: I call them the KCC's of listening. I use the initials BEE as a memory aid: being present, eye contact, and exchange (active).

Be Present. Imagine stepping into the office of *your* boss. You clearly want to talk and have something you want to get off your chest. You begin to explain your challenge, that you are struggling in moving a current project forward due to lack of priority within the organization.

It is obvious this is something that deeply concerns you and has occupied your mind. You are frustrated, need a sounding board, and are looking to your boss for a sympathetic ear and a second opinion.

Unfortunately, he/she refuses to look up when you start speaking, and continues to rearrange their desk, reply to an email, and/or conquer several social media posts. Their act of participating includes a few nods, short *hmmm*s, and okays.

At minimum, he or she is not looking at you, and worse, he or she has not put their bodily presence facing you and has not ceased multitasking. They have failed to give you their full undivided attention. As a result, you probably walk out of their office feeling a bit undervalued, confused, and wondering if you were making the issue more than it really was.

There is a more effective approach.

When an employee asks to speak to you, look at them with full eye contact and full facing body. Periodically acknowledge what they are saying, ask clarifying questions, and paraphrase. Once they are finished, ask if you might offer some suggestions.

Using the latter approach, they would leave feeling uplifted with a possible solution, acknowledged, and heard. Listening as a leader will instill a feeling of respect and value to your employees. In their mind, you cared enough to hit the pause button on your professional agenda, and to hear them out as not only employees but human beings.

Eye Contact. I mentioned eye contact as a key component of being present. I want to expand a bit more on the importance of eye gazing. How do you feel when someone you are talking to is looking away, at the door, or on their phone?

You don't feel like they care; you feel like they are disinterested in what you are saying, bored, or maybe not listening at all. Yet, how do you feel when someone is looking right at you, into your eyes, facing you? You immediately feel like they sincerely care, that what you are saying is important because their full attention is on you and your words of communication. You feel prioritized.

When people know they are being intently listened to by another, it actually creates a biochemical effect for us. Our brains release endorphins, making us *feel happy*. It raises our self-esteem and makes us feel good about ourselves as a person. The receptivity of our words and feelings by another person has an immense effect on us. When someone actively listens to us, acknowledges our words, asks questions, and restates our concerns, we naturally will trust and like the listener that much more. It is bonding.

When babies' and parents' eyes connect or *eye gaze*, it is the first emotional connection for a child. It is confirmation for the parents that the baby finally *sees* them and for the baby that they are important and recognized.

This developmental milestone is very significant in helping children develop capacities to feel calm and engage and relate to others. Has anyone ever said to you: "Hey, you are not paying attention to me"? It usually is because you are not looking into their eyes and are focused on something else. Eye contact is the strongest physical form of showing interest, and of *seeing* someone.

One of the easiest ways to become a better listener is to be a better eye gazer. Try it out and *see* how much more you feel engaged and connected to the other person and the other person to you.

Exchange (active). The final and third component to the *heart* of listening is what I call *active exchange*. Active exchange is not about you sharing your agenda or talking about yourself. The exchange is about you sharing, in words, what you *heard* the other person say or it is asking clarifying questions in order to restate what you have heard. Active exchange includes restating, paraphrasing, or empathizing what the other person has said. I use active exchange when I am consulting or coaching executives as it accomplishes two things: (1) that I have heard them correctly, and (2) that I understand what they have said.

The three options of restating, paraphrasing, or empathizing can be done as follows: Restating is simply stating back what someone has said. "So if I heard you correctly, you stated that the cost of this project, the ability to get it done in under six months, and to have the CFO's backing are the three most important factors in your decision to hire me for this project."

Another good technique is to paraphrase what someone has said, which is essentially repeating what someone has said but doing so in your own words. You will express the same ideas, but just in your own words, and usually in a compressed or condensed version. "So, the economic value, meeting an aggressive timeline, and having executive buy-in are your three biggest factors in selecting me for the project. Is that correct?"

Paraphrasing works really well in sales, or when someone is asking something of you that you need to make clear, as it truly shows that you have heard the person and have rephrased their needs using different words and restates their key decision points. Hearing what they have said can help ensure that they are being clear in their communication, as well.

Empathizing is simply stating the emotions or feelings that someone is stating or implying through body language and selected words. "I certainly can relate to the way you feel. There is a lot riding on the success of this project, so ensuring that value, an aggressive timeline, and your boss' approval are positively and strongly addressed with a partner you choose for this project, makes sense."

By truly listening and hearing what someone is saying, you are extending good will, enhancing connection, and achieving fulfilling engagement. This level of connection and engagement will be reciprocated when it is your turn to share.

In a final note: As a boss, leader, or executive, you *must* be aware of the possible emotions experienced by your employee when approaching you. Anyone stepping into your office to have a serious talk does so feeling one of several emotions.

- Trepidation is possible if they are asking for something like time off, a raise, or a promotion.

- Uncertainty is possible if they are not sure how well their point will be received. If they are voicing a complaint, some personalities will fear a reprisal. Others will wonder if they have lost credibility in your eyes, fearing they will be thought of differently.

In other words, an employee will rarely enter your office completely comfortable about speaking to you. Great leaders recognize this in advance.

A culture should be in place that eases these fears to some extent. They should know from past experience and word-of-mouth that you are very receptive to listening. If you have an open-door policy, set parameters, such as a time of day or day of the week, for these conversations to be freely permitted.

By scheduling the sessions, you control your time, can avoid someone being turned away when you aren't available, and show a willingness to discuss and listen.

Another foundational strategy for being a good listener is to interact with your employees often enough that a conversation is less ominous.

Ask yourself the following question: "How well do I know my team members or employees?" As you pass them in the hallway, do you know their name? Their spouse's name? Whether they have kids or not?

Most employees have a strong desire to please the boss. Perhaps just for job security but also because they see you as a mentor. When you show an appropriate interest in them and their lives, they will only respect you more, which will make conversations that much easier.

Connection Correction #5

The heart of listening requires not interrupting and listening without an agenda. To truly be a good listener, practice **BEE:** *Being present,* Eye *contact, and* Engagement *(active) by asking clarifying questions and sharing back what you heard.*

Chapter 5

Difficult Conversations And Conflict Resolution

"The way you communicate in challenging times dictates whether your organization thrives or barely survives."

—Michelle Mazur

Conflict at home or work is stressful and exhausting, regardless of how directly you are involved in the discussion. Unfortunately, conflict is ever-present as we are all human beings who have different needs and interpretations of our environment based on our own perspectives, perceptions, needs, and our past. The goal of effective conflict resolution is to come to an understanding of all sides, resolve the conflict at hand, and move forward positively with a best as possible win-win solution for all.

I see society becoming so adept at two-dimensional phone interaction that we are losing the ability to humanly engage and to resolve conflict. We choose to interact absent of personality, and generically via text, email, live chat, and websites. If we don't like the interaction, we may not respond, delete, unfriend, unlike, ghost, or swipe left. None of which would be acceptable in a face-to-face or phone-to-phone interaction.

These actions are not good demonstrators of conflict resolution, and certainly don't provide empathy for the other person. I will agree that it is much easier to send a text message or email with a message like, "You didn't get the job," or, "This is not working out," or maybe, "You can't come to the party," than delivering these disappointing messages in person, face to face, and real enough to see the other person's dejected posture and feel the recipient's hurt, disappointment, or upset emotions. When we avoid difficult conversations, we trade short-term discomfort for long-term dysfunction.

To illustrate the point, allow me to share another of my myriad of dating horrors. Once, an upstanding professional guy that I had been introduced to through a prestigious local business club, and with whom I had at least six dates that were absent of any indication that things were not moving forward, left me the following voicemail:

"Kimberly, I am sorry. I don't think we are a good match. I wish you the best, Matt."

What?

Again, this is a professional individual, with whom I have had at least six dates, and on both parts, there was perceived potential. It left me confused, angry, in disbelief, and ultimately with negative thoughts toward him. This was a mature adult male who was very successful in business but couldn't pick up the phone or meet me in person to have a respectable conversation and politely part ways and say goodbye.

How many of us are taking the easy emotional way out? If a person cannot have difficult conversations, are they suited for leadership? Leadership is about showing your values and integrity on your sleeve, and about leading by example, doing the tough stuff in full view of everyone else, not walking away from it.

Lately, amongst friends, I have seen relationships that have transpired three or more years, and one partner uses the vehicle of a text message to cut the cord. *Unbelievable.* This spineless action is disrespectful to what the relationship was, the time that was spent, the love that was shared, and a direct insult and slap in the face to the recipient. It takes strength, a spine, and integrity to communicate any uncomfortable issues at work or at home, face to face. It is the right thing to do and it cannot become a lost art. (Over my dead body, I would like to add.)

How do we create effective conflict resolution and have difficult conversations in the workplace and in all of our relationships? Is there a framework we can follow? Avoidance, anger, and control are not effective ways of managing conflict. Let's look at some easier ways to manage this problem.

KCC Four Dos For Difficult Conversations

The best thing I can say is, "Suck it up, buttercup," and have the spine to pick up the phone, or preferably ask to meet that person face to face. Try to come from a perspective that if you were the recipient of the bad news, how would you like to hear the news, and feel at the end of the conversation? Because it upset me greatly in the dating process when my prospective mate would fail to communicate to me in person or by a respectable phone conversation the end of our relationship, I vowed that in all of my dating situations, I would do what I valued. I can't say it was easy, and I can't say it was comfortable. But I can say I felt better about myself in communicating face to face, and it left me being clear that I was a good, kind, considerate person, and that goodness was usually reiterated by the recipient. Difficult conversations such as firing someone or ending a relationship or telling someone they are not a perfect fit for the job usually are around sharing bad news. That is nonnegotiable.

Here are the four dos for difficult conversations:

Nice And Neutral. Greet them nicely, in a neutral space where possible, and thank them for meeting you today.

Breathe. Take a big deep breath to center yourself.

Acknowledge The Person. Say, "I brought you here today . . ." or "I asked you to meet me in person, as I value (or respect) you as a person and human being."

Publish Your Statement. When I say *publish* your statement, I mean come up with a sentence that is not a question and is a firm expression of what you want to communicate. I also advise that you have come up with this statement and practiced it in advance. It is best when sharing disappointing information that is nonnegotiable to publish: make a clear, firm statement, absent of emotions and reasons. The more reasons you begin to include, the more it opens it up for a debate, which, at the end of the day, is futile in a nonnegotiable conversation. Also communicate using "*I*" *(the sole decision maker)*, or "*we*" *(the company, or group decision makers)*. Avoid making a "*you*" statement, which puts the other person on the defensive.

Here are some examples:

"I asked you to meet me in person as I value and respect you (our relationship, etc.). I have been thinking a lot about us and I have decided that I am not wanting to continue this relationship."

"Thank you for meeting me here today, as I respect and value you as a professional person. In the midst of our reorganization and downsizing, it has been decided that we have to let you go."

Try to keep any adjectives or emotions out of the statement, such as, "unfortunately," or "disappointingly" or "I'm afraid," as it already sets up the negative emotion for the recipient and you want to avoid putting emotions and feelings into their subconscious.

Again, try to avoid getting into the *whys* for the decision if this is a nonnegotiable decision. It only takes you down a rabbit hole that leaves both parties feeling uncomfortable and more hurt.

For example: "Why are we breaking up?" If I begin to share that there was no chemistry, or I didn't like his poor sense of humor, or he wasn't intelligent enough, etc., it will begin to wear on the other person's ego and hurt them even more.

You want to be able to allow that person to leave with dignity, so reiterating your published statement is a good option. "I really don't want to get into the details; it is best if we simply part ways."

Question: "Why didn't I get the job?" Answer: "We found a candidate that was a better fit for the position." Avoid getting into the finite, messy, subjective details that send you down a path of discomfort for both parties and provide poor closure.

I will leave this caveat: if this is a conversation around the end of a three-year relationship, the conversation may get very detailed and possibly, by being truly open, vulnerable, and honest about what you both feel, there is a possibility to work through the issues. My KCC Cliff's Notes for having difficult conversations is usually around less emotional connections between two people.

Connection Correction #6

Have those difficult conversations respectfully by picking up the phone or meeting them in person. Don't chicken out and use digital technology to manage your message impersonally. Be respectful to them as a human being, and suck it up, buttercup. You will feel better for having done so and so will they.

Okay, I have shared how to have difficult conversations that require you to share nonnegotiable information. Now let's look at the KCC Steps for Connected Conflict Resolution incorporating SPACE and SOLVE.

The KCC Keys To Correct Conflict Resolution

Resolving a conflict is never fun and sometimes can be emotional. Try to reduce the emotional charge by initially considering the acronym SPACE: separation, place, ask, collaboration, and elimination.

Separation. Allow at least twenty-four hours from initial point of conflict to first meeting and discussion so that initial reactive emotions simmer down.

Place. The place should be neutral ground. Schedule the meeting at a time that is conducive for all or most schedules, and make sure it is going to be conducted in a neutral zone (not someone's office), with minimal noise and distractions and a door that can be closed.

Ask. As in ask, don't demand. When you demand something from someone, you are trying to control them. Control is not a very productive approach and it immediately generates resistance. It is okay to sometimes come from a position of being in charge, but you should be guiding and advising, not demanding. By asking instead of demanding and incorporating a nonabrasive or soft tone without affronting or appearing to bully is key here. Technique and tone make all the difference in the world in how something is received.

Collaboration. Set the tone in all communication that this will be a collaborative effort with the goal of coming to a solution that resonates with everyone. We can also use the C for creativity. Invite everyone to come to the table with a creative mind and some out-of-the-box thinking in order to collaboratively resolve the issue at hand.

Elimination. Eliminate tenure and titles. Encourage all to leave their tenure and title in their office (including you) and to arrive with the true intent to listen to others as peers, and as true human beings with needs, fears, concerns, and emotions. It is important that this prep period conveys a safe environment, encourages individuals to take risks, and allows for people to truly say what they want to say without fear of a direct consequence.

Connection Correction #7

The heart of conflict resolution includes setting the stage proactively. Create **SPACE:** **S**eparation *between initial conflict; a* **P**lace *that is neutral and quiet;* **A**sk, *don't demand anything; let everyone know this is a* **C**ollaborative *effort; and* **E**limination *of any titles and tenures.*

The KCC Five Steps To SOLVE Your Conflict

On the day of the meeting, reiterate the SPACE objective. This is a sacred space, absent of titles and tenures, where we are collaboratively trying to come to a solution that resonates positively with everyone.

Designate someone to take minutes or ensure you have an executive assistant to do so. If you are not the facilitator, introduce the facilitator. Additionally, ask for someone to be the scribe on a white board or flip chart. Subsequently ensure you take pictures at the end of what has been written down.

Now walk through the following steps to SOLVE (state, objections, lay out, verify, and execute) on your area of conflict. This technique can be used when the conflict is between two or more people. Obviously, the greater the number of people, the longer it will take.

State. State the perceived issue or conflict. State and write down on the white board the current issue or statement that is creating conflict. Ensure that everyone agrees with the statement. As the leader, you might begin by stating, "I perceive that the issue that we have conflict over is . . ."

Example: "We have a deadline to submit this RFP/proposal by the end of the month (essentially four weeks). We must respond, as it is a key opportunity for significant business. The team feels that this is a very aggressive timeline considering all the pieces that need to be pulled together to create a solution. The team feels that this timeline will require working late every night and on the weekends in order to put together a thorough and quality driven proposal."

Objections. On a separate flip chart page, go around the room and write down everyone's objections to the issue and their feelings behind their objections.

Example: Bob, from finance, knows that typically it takes a minimum of four weeks to create all of the financials from every department related to cost and expenses to create the solution. This RFP and finance analysis is not the only one he is trying to complete. He has two others that have mutual significance. Sally from operations is struggling with defining the solution from a number of FTE requirements and skillsets in order to submit to Bob. Additionally, she feels we need more dialogue with the client in order to truly hone in on skill requirements for each FTE for this project and therefore billable rates. Which country we grab the labor from will also affect the skillset availability and the rates.

Lay Out. Lay out possible alternative (brainstorm) solutions. Have everyone go around the room and state possible alternatives:

- Can we ask the client for more time without being penalized?

- Can the other financial projects that Bob is working on push out their deadlines?

- Can Sally get more insight from the client regarding the solution to better hone in on number of FTE's and skillset requirements that will better help her define the solution and get it to Bob?

- If we can't get any more information from the client, can we possibly provide three solutions that utilize basic skillsets, moderate skillsets, and highest skillsets and propose a price range with factors of consideration?

Verify. Verify or vet which brainstorming ideas could work. This may require that you delegate a day or two for each idea to be vetted out by the individual who thought of it, or the individual who could most likely get the quickest answer. Questions to ponder: "In our time together, what would you like to see happen as a result or outcome of this meeting? What would be your ideal outcome? And, if that ideal outcome happened, what would that mean and look like for you?"

Execute. Bring everyone back together and report on what was possible. Regarding the possibilities laid out in step three:

- Can we ask the client for more time without being penalized? The answer from the client was no.

- Can the other financial projects that Bob is working on push out their deadlines? The answer from the other departments and leadership are "No."

- Can Sally get more insight from the client regarding the solution to better hone in on number of FTEs and skillset requirements that will better help her define the solution and get it to Bob? The client says, "No, that is all the information available at this time. More will come as the process unfolds."

- If we can't get any more information from the client, can we possibly provide three solutions that utilize basic skillsets, moderate skillsets, and highest skill sets and propose a price range with factors of consideration? In asking the client if it is okay to provide range pricing with the expectation there will be further discussion, the answer is yes.

Based on the client's feedback, it appears that Sally can create a three-tiered description of the operations, FTEs, and skillsets required to solve the problem that can be sent to Bob. Bob can use various rate cards and ranges already approved by finance and not have to go through the tedious and necessary approval process at this time. As Sally gathers more information, they can progressively build a case for finance.

Now we can move forward and execute on this collaborative win. The RFP gets submitted on time without compromising the company's chance to win the first selection of vendors.

If, for some reason, brainstorming solutions still create a gap between individuals and a collaborative solution cannot be reached, it might be necessary to bring in internal or external resources. Internal resources include human resources, ombudsman, or a panel. External resources include coaches and consultants who are experts in mediation and conflict resolution.

Connection Correction #8

Use my KCC methodology **SOLVE** *to solve your conflict.*
State *the initial premise, understand all* **O**bjections,
Lay out *and brainstorm ideas,* **V**erify *and* **V**et *the
brain-storming ideas, and* **E**xecute *your new solution.*

Chapter 6

The Lost Meal: The Hidden Power Of Breaking Bread

"The most valuable tool in our kitchen isn't found in any drawer or cupboard. It's the table."

—Julia Tushen

There's a great YouTube video titled #EatTogether2018, which shares my sentiments.

It shows the birth of a baby girl and illustrates how her entire life she is comforted by the love and community given and received when eating together.

It begins with the comfort of her mother's breast while breastfeeding as an infant. She then learns to feed herself by feeding others and progresses to childhood friendships over hot dogs and milkshakes. As a teenager, her team sports branch into team sharing of food and refreshments, and as a growing adult she continually enjoys the bonding experience of family dinners sharing french fries and eating off of each other's plates.

The entire segment and commercial hums to the tune of the Sonny and Cher classic and unmistakable "I Got You Babe." When watching, you experience the heartfelt warmth, joy, and importance of *breaking bread* with key people in her life. These are instrumental moments to her well-balanced development and connection from birth to adulthood.

It abruptly jumps ahead to a scene where she is now a working adult. She is on her lunch break and found eating her sandwich in a sterile office atmosphere, at her desk, alone. She is listening to "I Got You Babe" with her earbuds dangling and is surrounded by others doing the same.

The tagline reads: "We grow up eating together, why do we stop?"

Why do we stop?

We take sharing a meal for granted. We think it is a waste of time, that it is un-productive, and we are better served if we eat at our desk and plow through the next project outline, or the unread emails in our inbox.

We assume that it is not a necessity for our sustenance, or happiness. From a productivity standpoint, we assume that thirty minutes or an hour can be used in much more productive ways than sharing a meal with a potential client, colleague, or employee.

Imagine the information we could gather from these thirty-minute conversations, and more impressive will be the relationships and the connections that will ensue. Could you possibly have a better insight as to some of the challenges employees may be facing within your organization? Could you actually be able to identify your employees as human beings with families and interests outside of work? Do you think you might be considered more approachable and relatable if you did? Do you think you may be able to transfer some insight or mentorship to a soul over a meal? By incorporating this activity once a week, you will have potentially encouraged an employee to follow their dreams, discovered a new and creative way to build a culture of community, and/or endeared yourself as a real, vulnerable, and approachable leader.

"Nothing brings us together like eating together," according to the aforementioned *Oxford Economics* study. Eating meals together improves mood, combats feelings of isolation, and even improves self-image.

According to the study, someone who never or rarely ate their sit-down meals alone scored 7.9 points higher on a 100-point living well scale than someone who always or mostly ate their sit-down meals alone.

We consciously don't realize the power of sharing a meal. It is proven to make a significant difference in our wellbeing, and the wellbeing of those with whom we share it. When you share a meal, you are sharing a common pleasurable experience that bonds people together.

Maybe there was a great song playing in the background. Maybe the burger was the best burger you have had in years. Maybe it was a horrible downpour of a rainy day, but there was comfort in connecting over tea or coffee in a bistro café with a warm fire nearby. Eating together is an exponential experience. It is not just about the food; it includes the conversation, the shared atmosphere, the exchange of energy, and the ultimate connection.

Having a meal with a colleague, client, or employee immediately changes the energy and topics of conversation. When we sit down to break bread, it is naturally more permissible and we are more inclined to share personal anecdotes and reveal our vulnerability than when we are not. We will share a piece of ourselves while we share eating.

On the contrary, when we have our *initial* meetings in an office setting, our exchange is usually within the confines of office speak and business agendas. Rarely will it stray very far into personal conversations. However, if you have a second or initial meeting with that individual over coffee, or a meal, your conversation would be broadened to include personal interests and family, in addition to the business at hand. An energy exchange would occur, an experience would have been shared, and a deeper level of connection would have been created. The person across the table would be more of a human being than in its generic of forms, a means to advance your project, task, or agenda.

The connection and energy exchange from sharing a meal would transfer to the next time you met that individual in an office setting. It would be evident that there was now a human energy exchange going on versus just a business information exchange.

That is the power of breaking bread, and what I consider the lost meal. We all could feel better if we made more time to get together, eat together, and share together. I am cooking, so come on over. The door is always open.

We talked about the overall connections created when "breaking bread." In the next chapter we will get into why "breaking bread" is an important asset for your business.

Connection Correction # 9

Get out of your office and go break some bread. Begin by incorporating this once a month or once a week. A cup of coffee or lunch with a colleague, client, or an employee will be a powerful connection tool. Capitalize on the shared experience and shared energy that now builds a human connection versus a business interaction.

Honestly, I hate eating alone. I don't mind breakfast and lunch alone as I am usually conducting business with calls and meetings sporadically placed throughout the day. As a result, I eagerly look forward to dinner, my favorite meal, as it means relaxation, end of the workday, and a time to reflect. As a single person with no kids, it often consists of bread, butter, brie, and a bottle (my favorite chilled Chardonnay).

Yes, I fall into the statistic that I eat 19 percent or more of my sit-down meals alone, which is three times the national average. Sammy, my Shih Tzu, does believe himself to be handsome company, but he can't do that trick seven nights in a row. I will admit if I can't meet friends or don't have a networking meeting, one or two nights a week is tolerable, but by the third night I find myself anxious and seeking companionship and conversation.

Numerous studies have long suggested that we are social animals who gain major health benefits from connection (Singer 2019). That simple act of dining out and engaging in conversation immediately elevates my mood. Psychiatrist Robert J. Waldinger said: "Loneliness kills. It's as powerful as smoking or alcoholism."

And I have realized that by finding someone to share my dinner with, I am creating a simple fix to add camaraderie, connection, and community to my day.

I remember as a kid, I always looked forward to our family dinners as a time of gathering, good food, and an opportunity to share what transpired in our day for my myself, my two brothers, and my parents. Sometimes it was emotional, sometimes it was light and funny, but it was always connecting. I think that is why I have such a passion and comfort in cooking and baking. There is so much joy in the creation of the meal and even more so in the sharing of the food that was created. I see sadly today, with both parents holding down a career while kids' schedules are consumed by school, volunteering, and sports or social commitments, it can be extremely difficult to continue this necessary tradition. Eating together is an important and cultivating tradition that builds a home foundation of connection, conversation, and community.

In the video #Eattogether2017, a girl is at the end of her workday traveling home on the subway and being bumped and passed by. She reaches her apartment complex's crowded elevator and rides it to her floor amidst self-absorbed, in-a-hurry occupants. She exits the elevator to an empty apartment hallway and follows it to her apartment. When she arrives home, she finds her roommate preoccupied with her computer and failing to notice her entrance despite her loudly dropping her purse. In the background plays, "What the World Needs Now is Love Sweet Love" (written by Burt Bacharach and originally recorded by Jackie DeShannon in 1965).

The next scene has her and her roommate setting up tables and chairs in their apartment complex hallway complete with a table setting and food. As families and individuals exit their apartment, they are invited to join them and they too set up a table, chairs, and a home cooked meal. Soon the entire hallway is filled with all of the neighbors sharing food, laughter, and conversation, some appearing to have never really met before.

The final scene shows a young girl crawling beneath the row of tables to the end of the hallway where she knocks on the last door. Out comes an old man, and the two of them walk together hand in hand, radiantly, to join the hallway feast, as the lyrics "What the world needs now is love sweet love" gets louder. The tagline: "Nothing brings us together like eating together."

I feel we need to go back to incorporating the family dinner (even if it is takeout) as many times as possible to establish this important foundation. Additionally, as mentioned by one of my best girlfriends, it forces today's kids to learn how to communicate in full sentences. They also get an opportunity to express feelings, learn how to listen, and to be sensitive to others. As a busy executive, how often is your bucket being filled up with the presence of your family and loved ones around a dinner table? As a leader, leading with creating joy and connection at home is just as important as leading others in the workplace. As mentioned in my previous chapter, there is more to sharing a meal than simply the food. It is an all-out sensory orgy. Think about all of the senses that are engaged.

Please keep in mind that I am well aware of the five senses: smell, taste, sight, sound, and touch. With that being said, please enjoy my slight twist on the five by modifying touch to stimulus, and introducing a sixth:

The First Sense: Smell. From the minute you enter your mother's house on Thanksgiving with the comforting smell of roasted turkey, or you enter a samurai steakhouse and the scent of garlicy hot oil on the community grill fills your nostrils, your appetite is stimulated. Or it can be as simple as the local French café that emits whiffs of brewing coffee and the sweet buttery smell of warm pastries; it is the first sense activated in anticipation. The smells send your mouth watering and your lips smiling with the knowledge that you will be surrounded by others that are sharing and enjoying a common experience. You foresee connection.

The Second Sense: Taste. The texture and taste of our beverage, snack, salad, sandwich, or meal is a deciding factor as to our enjoyment. If it doesn't taste good, it is not likely we will remake or reorder. If it is too salty or too sweet, too bitter or too bold, too spicy or too saucy, our first taste will tell us whether we will finish what is before us or only go halfway. Tasting good food is an indulgent pleasurable experience.

The Third Sense: Sight. Today, so much of the appeal of our meal is based on the way our food is packaged, presented, and plated. Color, size, accents, trims, and plating all create a visual appeal that quickly turn us away or immediately has us picking up our fork. Some would argue that the packaging of a product is as important as the product itself.

The Fourth Sense: Stimulus. (Note: this sense is really touch, but for the purpose of this chapter and to illustrate the orgy of sensations when sharing a meal, I am modifying the fourth sense to stimulus.) Imagine a cute little Italian cafe, and upon your entry on this drizzly rainy day, a Dean Martin song is playing in the background and whiffs of rich coffee fill the air. Whether it is someone's home, a coffee shop, or a fine restaurant, you are usually changing your atmosphere when meeting someone for lunch, attending a dinner party, or having a business meal. This change a scenery brings on a freshness and an opportunity to alter your mood. A new stimulus! This new environment is full of new colors, scents, imagery, and noise, which add to the indulgence of our senses, pleasure, and positive feelings. It also creates a visual memory and sensation we can return to in our minds.

The Fifth Sense: Sound. The clinking of forks, the clinking of wine glasses, even the crashing of dropped dishes, coupled with the buzzing sounds of soothing conversation around us will fill us up from an auditory perspective and reiterate that we are not alone. Additionally, the act of being listened to significantly adds to the auditory value.

Now continue to flow with me as I introduce a sixth sense (a twist on the five senses) to illustrate the power of breaking bread.

The Sixth Sense: Chemistry. The sixth sense, in this book, is more of an abstract concept than a tangible one. It is analogous to the "chemistry" that is so undefinable between two lovers. Maybe not to that intensity, but there is a definitive energy exchange. "I am putting my love on your table," is a tagline that I use for my Live Life Lusciously Artisan Bakery (another one of my entrepreneurial endeavors. Live Life Lusciously is an ecommerce artisan bakery, www.livelifelusciously.com). I love to bake and cook so much that I believe that the love and nurturing sense I feel when baking actually gets transferred to my sweet treats. I use a few unique ingredients, always fresh and organic, but the same cream, butter, eggs, and sugar that every other baker uses. I am always thrilled when individuals that are not crazy about cheesecake or desserts always exclaim to their delight (and mine) how wonderful and tasty my desserts are "to die for!" It is why those that indulge in my Live Life Lusciously Italian mascarpone cheesecakes, luscious layer cakes, and perfect pies enjoy them so much. I believe there is a transfer of emotional energy that occurs when people share a meal together that would be absent if it was not in person.

There is an intangible chemistry that is shared by all who sit at the table and break bread together. Provided everyone is in good relations, the aura of energy, and the sharing of food enhance the feeling of connection and pleasure we get out of sharing a meal. It is an energy exchange. Hence why meeting someone in person reveals traits, likeability, or otherwise that cannot be predicted from a picture, resume, dating profile, or phone conversation. When I meet a potential client for lunch or dinner, there is that unexplainable energy exchange and bonding experience. Our conversation extends above and beyond my services and their needs, and we both walk away with more comfort and connection through the common experience, respect, and trust created and through shared some vulnerability.

Breaking bread with a potential client or even a colleague versus having a phone or Zoom video conversation has the potential to propel the relationship into a professional friendship that would be much more difficult and lengthier if attempted over digital technology.

Eating Together Is An Intimate Experience

My first husband was a bodybuilder. His dining preference was an all-you-can-eat buffet. He loved the fact you could fill your plate high and wide with a huge variety of options. His objective was to sit down and immediately consume his plate in order to joyously jump up for a second round. The running flavors of a buffet coupled with his fast-paced eating was so unfulfilling to me.

I dislike buffets, as the flavors of the multiple options seem to run together with no distinct taste (a sin to a good cook). Secondly, those items that are supposed to be hot are lukewarm and those items that are supposed to be cold are lukewarm. As a cook and baker, this was unacceptable.

Worse than the bleeding of lukewarm flavors was the lack of ambience when sitting in the cafeteria-like setting. And still least fulfilling and most significant was the absence of the benefits of sharing a meal: connection, conversation, and intimacy. Yes, I am a hopeless romantic, and needless to say, he wasn't, and I didn't stay married to him for very long.

I view eating as an intimate experience, and therefore, when dating, I rarely would accept an invitation to have lunch or dinner on my first date. I didn't want to have to try to enjoy my meal when my stomach is in knots or my date showed up not looking or reading anything like his profile and I knew there was not going to be a second date. On the flip side, when I was *in like* with someone, there was something very intimate when sharing a meal together—we possibly ate off each other's plates, fed each other tastes of what we thought were the most delicious part of our meal, or simply split all the courses.

While working for a large, well-known financial business process outsourcing company based in India, I was courting a healthcare client based in San Diego. Competition was tough, and internally, there was high visibility on this deal, and therefore on me. I was one of four companies selected after an RFP submission for this over $21 million deal.

As part of the decision making and final selection process, the client was to conduct a site visit to all four companies' outsourcing locations. In my case, it was Gurgaon, India, near Delhi and subsequently, Bucharest, Romania. The client representatives, Sue and Ted, met me in Gurgaon and we all stayed at the same place, the beautiful Leela Hotel. We spent the first two days of our visit, Thursday and Friday of that week, with long days in the office from eleven a.m. to midnight.

Prior to their arrival, the client had requested that we see one of the seven wonders of the world, the beautiful and majestic Taj Mahal, while in India. I thought this was a fabulous idea. However, what we were not prepared for was the incredible heat and humidity during the middle of August.

We left early on Saturday morning and embarked on the three-and-a-half-hour trek to Agra, the home of the Taj Mahal. I had arranged for a driver and a tour guide.

When we arrived, the opulent, domed mausoleum was as incredible as described. Unfortunately, as you can guess, it was not air conditioned and in this over 120-degree heat and high humidity, we all had constant drips of sweat running down every part of our bodies and felt smothered by the humidity. Additionally, Sue and I were draped in scarves and long pants to cover our bodies to honor the Indian religious customs. After six hours on the property, all four of us, including our guide, were ready to close out our tour.

A hot breeze from the van was better than no breeze. By the time we got back to the Leela, it was 6:30 p.m. At this point I was hot, tired, and extremely cranky, and by the looks on their faces, I knew that both Sue and Ted felt the same. The only thing that sounded good to me was to find myself a very comfortable seat in the air-conditioned lounge, and to relax with a chilled glass of Chardonnay.

After forty-eight hours in the office, and another brutal twelve hours in the heat of India, I anticipated that Sue and Ted would want to head back to their rooms. Especially given that they were flying out in less than six hours. Out of courtesy I invited them to join me in the lounge to wind down.

To my surprise they said, "Of course. We would love to."

We had the best time. Sue and I enjoyed a glass of chilled California Chardonnay while Ted had a classic Indian beer while we all indulged in various appetizers. The conversation was fun, light, and revealing as to the events of the last week. It was an enjoyable close to our client site visit.

We said our goodbyes so they could change and go to the airport and I closed out the bill. As I was getting up to leave, I was flooded by a good feeling and thought, "I got this." I felt that bonding time over the past three days between Ted, Sue, and myself created a professional friendship of trust and honesty that was necessary for them to make a final decision. We know people buy from people.

Within a month, I was notified that I was the vendor of choice, and in another three weeks, the deal was finalized. After that, I have never underestimated the power of connection, communication, and camaraderie over an event and a meal. Even though I am no longer at that company, I still value the opportunity to connect with my clients in person and over a meal in order to truly and sincerely create a partnership. To this day, I stay connected and are great friends with Ted and Sue.

Ted has even reached out to me to share the following: "Hey I just went through the cycle once again of the corporate proposal then site visits for three providers. I just wanted to tell you that even after doing this now three times, you are good at your job. I so wish we had someone like you supporting us on our vendor side right now. People are surprised when I tell them that all of us became good friends. Thanks Kim, you did and do a really good job."

I demonstrated that I sincerely cared, transparently communicated, actively listened, and created opportunities for true connection. Breaking bread was a key part of that relationship.

In the next chapter, I will provide a framework for introducing a culture of connection and improving your employee engagement.

Connection Correction #10

If you want to build a real connection with someone, create a shared experience over breaking bread. It is one of the best tools for an executive, and especially a sales executive. One good meal and time together will beat out twenty Zoom meetings or phone calls in a heartbeat.

Chapter 7

A Corrected Connected Course

"We must establish a personal connection with each other. Connection before content. Without relatedness, no work can occur."

—*Peter Block*

I shared with you several tools in the previous chapters that can help build connection within your organization as a leader. This chapter will highlight several practices you can incorporate within your organization to continue to build a sense of belonging, to demonstrate appreciation for your employees as human beings, and create accessibility as a leadership team.

After being awarded the outsourcing business from the San Diego-based healthcare company I talked about in the last chapter, I began the process of helping them transition their workforce from their corporate entities to ours. As a result, I was on their corporate campus three to four days a week and connected with their leadership team often. I was very impressed with their CFO, who in my mind, did not act like a typical CFO—aloof, introverted, and one-dimensional.

This CFO was engaged, extroverted, and multi-faceted. He was obviously highly intelligent, but he also had a great sense of humor and was quite open, available, and visible as a leader. I admired him as a person, a leader, and for the corporate culture he created.

Not only was he accessible, he was committed to making a difference. Every spring and fall he would sell tickets to eager employees to create their unique paintball team. The employee paintball team would have the fun luxury of shooting their paintball ammunition at the executive leadership paintball team while running through the hills of San Diego. Funds were collected and donated to a charity of the company's choice. It was a half-day corporate event complete with food, refreshments, fun, and music.

At the next town hall, the CFO would announce the amount of money that was raised for the designated charity. Additionally, he would show highlights of the day's fun with a myriad of videos and pictures from the colorful and dynamic paintball fight, along with candid photos of employees at the social gathering. It was an event in the company that everyone looked forward to. It also was an event where titles and tenure didn't matter. On the paintball field, all were equal: shooting colorful paint at each other, and having a blast.

Connection Correction #11

Find a charity that the company supports and build a fun event around raising money for the charity that breeds equality, fun, and community.

Because we spend so much time at work, I am seeing a movement for organizations to also create wellness and educational activities that address the needs of their employees outside of work within corporate time spent. For example, yoga instructors and dietitians are asked to come in and to conduct classes that talk about nutrition, mental and spiritual balance, and managing stress. Depending on your employee population and life experiences, I have seen companies bring in speakers to discuss: "How to Buy a Home," or "How to Shop for the Right Mortgage," or "How to Set Yourself Up for Retirement Success."

These are all educational tools that bring employees together and also recognize that employees have needs outside of work. By solving some of your employees' life challenges, you are (1) reducing their inherent stress that accompanies these issues, and (2) enabling them to have greater focus and productivity at their jobs. Importantly, too, you are acknowledging them as human beings with lives outside of work.

Connection Correction #12

Provide wellness opportunities such as yoga or meditation to relieve employee stress, and/or educational sessions that target stressful issues employees face outside of work, such as homebuying or finding the right mortgage.

The last two years as an executive in my corporate career were for a startup that provided customer service as an outsourcing service by leveraging the gig economy. The platform supported its clients with a customer service delivery model that pulled from a pool of trained customer service representatives who worked from home either part-time or full-time.

Statistics show that working from home is much more acceptable than say ten years ago. For those in management, business, financial operations, and professional jobs, it can be 35-38 percent of the employee population. The future anticipates that 68 percent of United States workers will be enjoying this freedom. Not relegated to high tech start-ups, permitting employees to work from home is now a working environment employed by traditional employers.

The freedom to do business anywhere provided by technology, coupled with the significant reduction in overhead costs from the elimination of office space, certainly support this trend and make it a winning argument. Additionally, it offers positive improvements in stress, wellbeing, and overall job satisfaction for most employees. Working from home allows for increased flexibility. Studies show that this increased flexibility results in increased gratitude and job satisfaction for working parents, along with decreased stress.

However, employers and employees need to also recognize that this model is not ideal for everyone who desires flexibility and a shorter commute. A work-from-home opportunity may at first appear to be an opportunity for freedom and flexibility, but for some it can then turn into a misfortune of loneliness, isolation, and depression. This isolation and its adjoining depression can materialize into lower productivity, not higher, in comparison to those that flourish in this environment. One study shows that 21 percent of remote workers named "loneliness" as one of their main on-the-job issues when working from home in addition to feeling a lack of community (source "State of Remote Work 2018," https://open.buffer.com/state-remote-work-2018/#benefits).

If employers and employees still wish to have the flexibility of working from home, it may be a nice balance to introduce an in-the-office day, whereby remote employees are encouraged to come into the office. When remote workers choose to venture into the office at least once a week, they are reportedly happier with a slightly higher rate of engagement. They are also more likely than full-remote or full-office workers to acknowledge they have a best friend at work, and their work allows for continued learning and growth.

As a leader, it is important to reach out to these remote employees on a regular basis. This reach out needs to be individualized and separate from the weekly team call. In my last executive role, our team was missing this action from our leader. As a result, we created our own regular points of connection within the team, absent of our leader. It became quite clear that the more and more our leader became successful and powerful, the less engaged he was with our team. He quite frankly did not care about us as individuals or human beings and had sole interest only in our outputs that contributed to his success. He was a very poor example of leadership, and one of the reasons I eventually left. Don't be that type of leader; actively demonstrate true interest in your team, individually and collectively, otherwise all they will feel is indebted servitude.

Weekly team calls are great for the sense of community and belonging to a team and are imperative. These weekly team calls can be enhanced with in-person meetings monthly or quarterly. Conducting in-person meetings for a day or two are critical to keep your team motivated and humanly connected by sharing successes and challenges. It also helps to prevent burnout and staleness.

Individual meetups over a cup of coffee or lunch periodically, or at minimum, a phone call with an individual employee that goes beyond the discussion of project updates and work-related conversations, can carry a lot of weight in employee esteem, connection, productivity, and loyalty.

As leaders, the more we act like we care, and sincerely and genuinely do, the more our employees will be more willing to take risks, put in their best effort on a deadline, inspire with creative ideas, and contribute positively and greatly.

Connection Correction #13

When leveraging a work-from-home environment, advocate for employees to come into the office once a week. Schedule monthly or quarterly team meetings, and weekly individual meetings in person or over the phone. Minimally check in with your direct reports above and beyond projects, deadlines, and sales quotas.

Business and corporations can be so focused on productivity, quality, and the bottom line that they negate their best asset: the human essence of their employees.

We analyze and scrutinize and set activity requirements for productivity. We implement technology to help employees do their jobs faster and more efficiently. We streamline management teams and let go of potential excess positions in an effort to force employees to be more productive while reducing costs. We have maxed out on organizational restructuring, downsizing, and implementing innovative technology.

It's time to max in on your best asset, the human essence of your employees. Employees are human beings, and I feel businesses sometimes lose sight of that in the pursuit of the almighty profitable dollar.

Yes, business must be profitable or there will be no business to employee people. But, sterilizing an employee down to productivity and quality numbers, and an employee ID loses sight of the true value of the power of many human beings working toward a common theme and goal. It is exponential. When we start treating our employees as human beings and not output machines, we will get more output out of the human being than we would the machine.

As leaders, we need to go beyond the interest of the project, business agenda, and financial spreadsheets and pull in the mindset of the employee through sincerity, genuine interest, and paying attention to them as a person.

Don't be one of those leaders who isn't listening, and who is broken off from their ability to relate. Be sensitive to the stress on employees and their families certain projects require. For example, for an individual who travels extensively with many hours on planes, trains, and automobiles, outside of an eight-to-five, don't plan four meetings the day they return. Be considerate and give them the freedom to come in a bit later or the next day in order to regroup and recharge with their families. The time away granted to recharge and your sincere concern create a productive, happy, and engaged employee. In moments like these, true sincere interest, sensitivity, and compassion can go a long way for creating an environment of community, loyalty, and engagement—something that is missing in a lot of organizations today.

Connection Correction #14

Start treating employees as human beings, not output machines, and you will get more output out of your human beings.

As a leader, one of your intrinsic responsibilities is to help grow and develop your people. Part of that is knowing what your employees' goals are and help them work toward achieving them.

You can increase their exposure to the associated duties with their goal by having them test out certain responsibilities. Maybe you give them an opportunity to lead a meeting once a quarter for them to develop their presentation skills. Or, maybe you have them facilitate a discussion on the new project assigned to your team.

A very successful way to grow your employees is to institute a mentorship program. Your company's mentorship program can consist of seasoned leaders who can help coach, educate, and demonstrate key qualities and expertise for those aspiring to be in those positions. Mentoring is a great tool to connect tenured skilled employees with those newcomers that are looking for a buddy who can help them get to the next level, and a resource to get answers outside of their boss.

When creating opportunities for growth and development, as a leader, keep in mind to leave your ego at your desk. Often, as leaders, we feel threatened if someone is smarter, more certified, more degreed than we are. They could have significant achievements or get promoted to a great position. Instead of absorbing it as a threat, acknowledge it as a complement to your ability to lead and excel at your career. Pat yourself on the back, in a humble way, and realize you have connected with that employee and made a significant difference in their growth, development, and success.

Connection Correction #15

Make your employees' growth and development a key responsibility: (1) provide ongoing opportunities to grow their skillsets, (2) create a mentorship program, and (3) celebrate your employees' promotions and wins as a reflection of your awesome skills as a leader.

How many leaders do you know who consciously create a line of separation and division between themselves and those below? Their pompous prowess around the office, political power games, manipulating agendas, and management by fear all create a barrier. Because they have a title, they believe they have respect and are a great leader. Not always the case. Do you help your people grow? Do you bring out the best in your people or the worst? Do you acknowledge others or steal their accomplishments?

Moving forward, leave your title on your desk, and start becoming a part of your organization by connecting using transparency, regular communication, breaking bread, and active listening.

Incorporate the following on a regular basis:

Recognize and reward individuals. It doesn't have to always be big bonuses and monetary remuneration, personally contacting an employee with a phone call or better yet, an in-person visit will put their level of appreciation and value through the roof. Make it a tradition to recognize employee achievements or above and beyond efforts at town hall meetings and visible employee boards.

Empower others to decide. Often, because we are ultimately accountable for a project, or outcome, we don't empower our employees to take the risks and challenges necessary to grow. We end up doing the heavy lifting by ourselves and take all the credit. Learn to spread engagement to employees through empowerment, and small challenges to shine. You are building their sense of belonging and contributing in addition to helping them grow into the position they are meant to be. Along the same lines of empowering others is to know your strengths and weaknesses.

Delegate to others. Delegate those tasks and responsibilities to employees that excel and can perform them better than you. It is a sign of a great leader who is not threatened by the better capabilities of others. It is also acknowledging that you are human and not infallible. You will convey a certain level of transparency that is critical for connection and what we have discussed so much throughout this book.

Don't micromanage your people. You don't like it nor do they. Release your need to control and instead permit a level of freedom and creativity. Creating this freedom must be a foundational part of your culture along with trust and safety to take risks. You can support this by recognizing and rewarding creativity and new ideas, even if they don't always pan out. There are many ways to accomplish the same task and just because you always did it one way, doesn't mean a new perspective and path can't be revealed. Additionally, it allows employees to find their own way, fail, and try again for the ultimate reward of success. You may also want to consider allowing certain decisions to be made without necessarily always having prior approval.

All of the above will take some pressure off of you and noticeably create improvements in productivity and office morale.

Connection Correction #16

Leave your title at your desk and start recognizing and rewarding individuals for creativity, stellar skillsets, and small and large accomplishments. Empower employees to solve problems and to lead change instead of doing it all yourself.

At the close of this chapter and this book, I will leave you with this one final thought. With our busy lives, demanding careers, dynamic families, and rush to do and balance everything, we are choosing to rely on digital technology to solve many of our problems, to complete our tasks, and to predominantly communicate. I say we need to consciously *stop!*

Going back to the reason I wrote this book, we are all moving consciously or more so subconsciously, toward being more broken off. Science is even proving it and calling it a dangerous and growing epidemic.

At the 125th Annual Convention of the American Psychological Association, Julianne Holt-Lunstad from Brigham Young University presented the results of 148 studies with a total of 308,849 participants. The study laid out the connection between loneliness (and I throw in disconnection, lack of belonging to a community, and isolation) and premature mortality. "There is robust evidence that social isolation and loneliness significantly increase risk for premature mortality, and the magnitude of the risk exceeds that of many leading health indicators," Holt-Lunstad shared.

I ask you as leaders to begin changing this epidemic by first affecting your own circle of influence, your employees, and your personal and professional relationships. We need to consciously choose to take more time, and to choose the human way. It does not have to be all the time, but at least three times a day as we discussed in my KCC three daily touchpoints. Pick up the phone instead of texting; schedule an in-person meeting versus an email; and have that family dinner once a week. If we don't, I believe we are doing ourselves, our families, and our relationships a disservice. It is too easy these days to be digital and task-oriented versus being humanly analog and connection inspired. Be vulnerable, be present, truly listen to understand, and break some bread.

The KCC Connection Corrections

Connection Correction #1. What secret are you hiding? What story are you not telling? What lie are you holding on to? Nathaniel Branden said: "When we bury our feelings, we also bury ourselves. It means we exist in a state of alienation. We rarely know it, but we are lonely for ourselves." By not revealing what you are burying, hiding, or lying about, you are not fully being present. Therefore, you are not showing up with all of you and the best version of yourself, as a leader. Your vulnerability is the best, most relatable part of yourself. Find a friend, colleague, medical professional, spiritual or religious advisor you trust to reveal, to embrace, and to accept this part of yourself and be on your way.

Connection Correction #2. What is missing in your corporate culture to drive employee retention and engagement? Interview your employees to find out if they feel valued and respected, that their work and their contributions make a difference, and they feel safe to take risks in thoughts, ideas, and in action. Is there a sense of belonging?

Connection Correction #3. As a leader or executive, what vulnerability, story, or relatable aspect of yourself can you share with your team and your employees that will make you less perfect and more liked? Try it out on your immediate team and see the results. Then try it out on a larger audience. When we risk being authentic, we gain connection, engagement, joy, and success.

Connection Correction #4. Introduce *mobile-free meetings* at least once a week. Introduce *mobile-free meals* at least once a week at home, and in all business meals, where possible. Exercise three points of connection a day, where you opt to exercise your ability to create human connection versus using digital technology by calling, meeting in person, or sharing a meal.

Connection Correction #5. The *heart of listening* requires not interrupting and listening without an agenda. To truly be a good listener, practice **BEE:** *Being* present, *Eye* contact, and *Engagement* (active) by asking clarifying questions and sharing back what you heard.

Connection Correction #6. Have those difficult conversations respectfully by picking up the phone or meeting them in person. Don't chicken out and use digital technology to manage your message impersonally. Be respectful to them as a human being, and suck it up, buttercup. You will feel better for having done so and so will they.

Connection Correction #7. The heart of conflict resolution includes setting the stage proactively. Create **SPACE**: *Separation* between initial conflict; a *Place* that is neutral and quiet; *Ask,* don't demand anything; let everyone know this is a *Collaborative* effort; and *Elimination* of any titles and tenures.

Connection Correction #8. Use my KCC methodology **SOLVE** to solve your conflict. *State* the initial premise, understand all *Objections, Lay out* and brainstorm ideas, *Verify* and *Vet* the brainstorming ideas, and *Execute* on your new solution.

Connection Correction #9. Get out of your office and go break some bread. Begin by incorporating this once a month or once a week. A cup of coffee or lunch with a colleague, client, or an employee will be a powerful connection tool. Capitalize on the shared experience and shared energy that now builds a human connection versus a business interaction.

Connection Correction #10. If you want to build a real connection with someone, create a shared experience over breaking bread. It is one of the best tools for an executive, and especially a sales executive. One good meal and time together will beat out twenty Zoom meetings or phone calls in a heartbeat.

Connection Correction #11. Find a charity that the company supports and build a fun event around raising money for the charity that breeds equality, fun, and community.

Connection Correction #12. Provide wellness opportunities such as yoga or meditation to relieve employee stress, and/or educational sessions that target stressful issues employees face outside of work, such as homebuying or finding the right mortgage.

Connection Correction #13. When leveraging a work-from-home environment, advocate for employees to come into the office once a week. Schedule monthly or quarterly team meetings, and weekly individual meetings in person or over the phone. Minimally check-in with your direct reports above and beyond projects, deadlines, and sales quotas.

Connection Correction #14. Start treating employees as human beings, not output machines, and you will get more output out of your human beings.

Connection Correction #15. Make your employees growth and development a key responsibility: (1) provide ongoing opportunities to grow their skillsets, (2) create a mentorship program, and (3) celebrate your employees' promotions and wins as a reflection of your awesome skills as a leader.

Connection Correction #16. Leave your title at your desk and start recognizing and rewarding individuals for creativity, stellar skillsets, and small and large accomplishments. Empower employees to solve problems and to lead change, instead of doing it all yourself.

Appendix B

A Brief History Of Leadership

"To handle yourself, use your head; to handle others, use your heart."

—Eleanor Roosevelt

What kind of leader do you aspire to be?

Think back to the various types of leaders you have dealt with or worked under thus far and make a mental list under two headings: effective and ineffective. Then place the leaders into each category.

When doing this, detach your personal opinion of them as people and set aside ideas or policies that you would have preferred them to use.

Keep it simple and analyze whether or not they were effective. Study the list of leaders you placed into the effective category and focus on what made them effective. Was it simply the decisions they made or was their effectiveness based more on their leadership style?

Now look at the other list. Try to arrive at a single reason that best summarizes their ineffectiveness. What can you learn from this?

Leadership is a vital skill. It takes place all around us to various degrees of efficacy every day. If you aspire to be a leader, or perhaps ascend to a higher rung on the leadership ladder, visualize yourself in the leadership role you hope to hold one day.

Envision you celebrating your one-year anniversary in that role.

How will the people you lead define you, as successful or a failure? Do you only care about results? Do you want them to like you, too? Is creating a stable, safe work culture important to you? Would you want to work for or with you?

If we were to poll one million future leaders and ask them what would make them successful in a leadership post, there would assuredly be a wide variety of answers.

Many leaders would feel successful merely by making a company more profitable, while others would point to metrics involving nationwide growth or opening additional locations. Yet, when a company is struggling, a new leader is brought in and can be deemed successful by laying off workers, shuttering stores, and stopping the financial bleeding.

Outside of the business world, leadership takes on a different hue.

In Major League Baseball, a manager can be seen as a great leader based on the number of games they win, their in-game tactics, or by how they steer their team through an unforeseeable tragedy.

Whereas the manager of a Little League team of eight-year-olds should be measured differently, such as by their ability to help young players improve and ensuring that the players had a lot of fun.

The mayor of a town can measure success in a multitude of ways. If they create more jobs for their residents, reduce crime, improve the schools, or gentrify bad neighborhoods many people will tout their success.

This brings us to a harsh reality that applies to everyone in a leadership role. Most leaders will never be unanimously loved. In this example, the same mayor will have critics who point out the things they *failed* to do as proof they were a poor leader.

In an increasingly divisive society, that is an unfortunate truth with no easy solution.

Many different types of leadership exist and many of them have labels such as servant leaders, participatory leaders, or authoritarian leaders. Though results are the most typical measure of success or failure, there is another side to leadership that should not be overlooked: the impact on the people they serve.

A Brief History Of Leadership

Let's look back at a brief history of leadership.

Dating back several millennia, societies lived as tribes. These groups were led by chieftains, which eventually became known as chiefs. As the centuries passed, tribes became less nomadic and built the early versions of cities. As civilizations sprouted, the names of the leader morphed into things like king, queen, emperor, czar, sultan, and many other titles.

These leaders ruled with absolute authority and if the people under them disagreed with decisions or policies, it was in their best interests to keep it to themselves. The majority of the time humans have lived on Earth, laws weren't codified, and the leader served as judge and jury.

There was no such thing as appeals.

The iron-fisted leadership style received its first dent in 1649 when King Charles I of England was beheaded after losing the English Civil War. Charles I, believing he had Divine Right—or permission from God—to rule, protested as such during his trial.

To no avail.

He was executed on January 30 by beheading.

This was unprecedented. A king claiming "Divine Right" was nothing new, but the people had reached their limit and chose to execute their leader.

This uprising caused rulers throughout Europe to shudder at the possibility that their own people could rebel and win.

Charles I's execution gave the people a tiny taste of control and a desire for more of it, which led to absolute monarchies giving way to constitutional monarchies, which was a small step forward.

For the common people, having a king controlled by a constitution offered a modicum of freedom and protection from some governing abuses. By appeasing the people a little, this olive branch also offered the reigning kings a buffer zone from their own beheading.

The success of the US revolution against the mighty British Empire served as a flashpoint that motivated dozens and dozens of revolutions worldwide over the next fifty years. About a decade later, in 1793, King Louis XVI of France became the only French king to ever be executed.

His death, and the rise of the French people, shook the rulers of neighboring countries.

They feared the beliefs and spirit of the French people would spread like an intellectual contagion to their own populations. This led to an unusual cooperation amongst ruling families who didn't care for one another, but all shared in the desire of self-preservation.

As each revolution took place, populations gained more and more freedoms while national leadership saw its power being increasingly controlled.

More changes took place at the end of World War I as the losing countries endured leadership changes along with the loss of land and resources. The Treaty of Versailles' punitive nature led to the rise of authoritarian dictators like Adolf Hitler and Benito Mussolini.

Authoritarian rule can lead to rampant abuse of the people in a society, which is why the term "dictator" carries a negative connotation. Even though there are examples of such leaders who didn't abuse their unchecked power, they are the exception.

To present this accurately, it should be noted that there are times when authoritarian, sometimes called totalitarian, rule is quite effective. Typically, this is in time of national emergency or during a war.

Even the US President can suspend part or all of the Bill of Rights, as proven with The Sedition Act of 1918.

The brutal actions of these dictators, and others like them, served as a modern example for people everywhere of life without rights. After their defeat in World War II, many countries swung further toward empowering people. As the decades passed, more laws protected the rights of citizens, workers, and minorities in many countries around the world.

So, it has been a long and painful rise to respectability and fair treatment for citizens and employees around the world.

Why the history lesson?

Because today's wide-ranging societal expectations are built upon that long struggle. Even if the bulk of employees or citizens don't know or understand that history, they have certainly grown comfortable with how they are treated today.

Perhaps entitled in some cases.

Regardless, people living and working in modern societies with protected rights aren't going to relinquish that treatment; and they won't happily accept heavy-handed treatment in the workplace or anywhere else.

Examples Of Business Leadership

With that as a backdrop, let's look at some well-known examples of leadership through the actions of prominent leaders.

Bill Gates of Microsoft and Steve Jobs of Apple enjoyed rousing success. Their companies became global technology linchpins and their stockholders benefited tremendously.

Once again, successful leadership can be a moving target of sorts. In many ways, these two men are the definition of success, but they weren't easy to work for at times.

Should the opinions of their employees matter? The stockholders may not care, nor do the bulk of the people buying and using their products.

But the employees did.

Could the same level of success have been attained with a more employee-friendly tact? We will never know. Perhaps only their hard-charging style extracted the very best from their employees. Or, would a more relaxed environment have been even more conducive to creativity?

The more public the role, the more important certain skills become. President John F. Kennedy and Dr. Martin Luther King, Jr. were both outstanding orators and were able to lead in part through charisma.

In his inauguration speech, President Kennedy's famous quote, "Ask not what your country can do for you, ask what you can do for your country," set the tone for his presidency. His "Ich bin ein Berliner" speech in West Berlin, just months before his assassination, gave the German people in that free half-city some comfort during a tense military crisis.

King proved that upending the status quo could be done peacefully. His movement was also powered by his great speaking ability. His "I Have a Dream" speech is famous the world over and undoubtedly helped draw attention to his efforts long after his assassination.

King was also an example of a servant leader, one that works to improve the situation of their followers. Servant leaders aren't chasing a new product release, corporate earnings, or the largest corner office.

Walt Disney and Jobs were both known to roll up their sleeves and work alongside their employees. Their participation in the work they oversaw demonstrated their commitment to detail and genuine love for their products.

Doing so had to leave an impression on the employees tasked with developing and improving the products. These men weren't dispatching orders from Wall Street; they loved the hands-on work of developing their products and brands.

Arianna Huffington built the *HuffPost* into a wildly successful and popular online platform for blogging and political news. Though she created an incredible product, it came at a cost: her own health.

After collapsing from exhaustion in 2007, she pivoted to a view more aligned with a good work/life balance. In an interview with *Director Magazine*, she described her leadership philosophy this way: "Both my own leadership style, and that of the other leaders at *HuffPost*, is very much like being in the middle of the circle, rather than at the top of the mountain shouting down" (Maxwell 2014).

Huffington added: "Leaders need to find that place of wisdom, strength, and real connection (with themselves and others) and they need to lead from that place."

Huffington also challenged the status quo with her views on productivity and the treatment of her employees. She installed several nap rooms and encouraged employees to schedule an opportunity for a quick restorative break during the workday.

HuffPost employees are also never to be involved with work emails after hours or over the weekends.

From a *Forbes* interview, Huffington stated: "Ninety-nine percent of the time it's not urgent and to create a culture where you are constantly plugged in and expected to be always-on is to create a culture of a burnout."

Huffington isn't the only famous leader that made a good impression. Gates lead by example when flying coach with several other Microsoft employees as detailed in a 2014 article by Julie Bort for *Business Insider*, when Brad Silverberg, a Microsoft SVP, was quoted as saying:

Shortly after I had joined Microsoft in 1990, Bill, I, and a few others on the Windows team were flying to NY from Seattle for some customer meetings. This was shortly after the launch of Windows 3.0. Though this was almost twenty-five years ago, Microsoft was a public, prosperous company. Yet, company policy was that everyone flew coach. And there was Bill, sitting in coach, in a middle seat. It didn't matter to him; he spent the whole flight reading. He wasn't as universally recognized then, so it wasn't such an issue for him to fly commercial. It made a big impression on me, a new Microsoft employee, seeing Bill lead by example (Burt 2014).

This shows that many leaders can display differing attributes. Though Gates was a difficult boss in his early years, he is now an unparalleled philanthropist. He and his wife Melinda have donated tens of billions of dollars to charities fighting diseases and aiding education worldwide. They have been lauded as one of the top fifty most powerful leaders in the world by *Fortune* magazine.

Academy Award winner Jordan Peele, another *Fortune* magazine honoree, has left his mark in Hollywood as a director. Rather than having a myopic view of his career, he is accepting open script submissions. Doing so allows his production company to help unknown filmmakers of all backgrounds gain traction in an industry where doing so is very difficult.

On a less-prominent level, there are examples of good leadership all around us. The founders of Bombas socks donate a pair of socks to charities for the homeless for every pair they sell, as does the shoe retailer Toms.

Critics may accuse them of using altruism to boost sales, but charities benefit in the end.

Zoom out further and people may love the pastor of their congregation, their child's history teacher or dance instructor, or their own boss.

At the state and local level, government executives are no stranger to scandals and orange jumpsuits either.

As an example, the state of Illinois has sent two governors to prison since the year 2000.

Retired Penn State assistant football coach Jerry Sandusky was sent to prison in 2012 on forty-five counts of child molestation and variety of church officials have stained their congregations with similar crimes.

Newsworthy scandals are far from the only example of leadership shortcomings.

Though coaches may draw the ire of their fanbase for this reason or that, ultimately, they may be doing as good as they are capable of.

Fulfilling one's leadership potential doesn't necessarily portend success. That level may still result in failure.

Typical examples of failed leadership involve caving to temptations, abuse of power, bad decision-making, vacating moral obligations, or violating a civic trust, more than getting outsmarted on fourth and goal from the one-yard line.

On that note, the National Football League has written guidelines for franchises thinking of relocating from one city to the next. The policy states: "Article 4.3 also confirms that no club has an 'entitlement' to relocate simply because it perceives an opportunity for enhanced club revenues in another location" (*2019 NFL Rulebook*. Retrieved from https://operations.nfl.com/the-rules/2019-nfl-rulebook/).

Yet, when St. Louis Rams owner Stan Kroenke wanted to move his team to Los Angeles, league owners voted overwhelmingly to allow the move despite the city of St. Louis jumping through each hoop the NFL laid in front of them to keep the team in St. Louis.

Having a written policy, then overlooking it, invalidates every written policy they have and is the definition of bad leadership.

The most combustible element poor leadership can create is an environment of widespread resentment from their staff. This may stem from the leader focusing on the fact that they are in charge, and not on the people they are leading.

Any leader who, over an extended period of time, is frequently reminding others that they sit atop of the chain-of-command has lost their way.

And resentment will soon begin to boil.

Team members and employees won't always have the optimal makeup and character, but they assuredly know who the boss is every day when they arrive at work.

Verbal reminders, such as "I am in charge here" or "I make the decisions here," may be necessary on occasion but certainly indicate a culture problem that needs to be rectified.

Most certainly, such declarations can be restated to deescalate the situation and frame the circumstances in a way the employee understands.

So often an effective leader's people skills can mediate a situation and prevent a situation from becoming inflamed. Though people skills often relate to a person's skill at communicating and explaining situations to another person or group, a leader's actions can also fall into that category.

An example: A school district has fallen on hard times financially. By every metric, the district is successfully educating its students, but the tax base has changed. Revenues are down as the time teachers' salaries are to be negotiated approaches.

To be fiscally responsible, the district cannot offer a raise to all teachers across the board, if revenues cannot support. Unfortunately, the school district tells the teachers that their salaries will be frozen for the upcoming year. No raises for anyone.

Not only does that cause salaries to, in effect, decline slightly due to cost-of-living increases, it also has a negative impact on the teachers' pension after retirement.

No staff members are happy but, being highly educated, many understand that the district cannot afford raises.

Then word gets out that the superintendent of the district got a big raise.

In most cases, teaching staff are paid from a different financial pool than administrators. That superintendent's raise was negotiated in his or her contract. The bump in pay will happen regardless of the district financial status.

That could be described as good negotiating and being tone deaf at the same time.

In that example, the teachers, who make a direct daily impact on the district's purpose of educating children, receive no pay increase, but they watch their boss, who rarely interacts with the students, walk away with a five-figure increase in salary.

How will that impact the mood of the workplace?

The superintendent is entitled to the money their contract guarantees them, but where is the leadership?

Now imagine that exact scenario unfolding with only one wrinkle of difference. The superintendent proactively tells his staff that, though he or she has a big raise coming, they will refuse to accept a raise until the teachers can also enjoy one.

Which scenario will create a more loyal employee base? To which of those superintendents will the faculty relate to better and admire more?

Now let's dissect another scenario.

Again, the teachers will receive no raise due to revenue shortfalls. The superintendent, eager to protect the positive climate and culture of the employees, eschews the raise as indicated before.

But they also take another step.

After explaining the unfortunate financial predicament, the superintendent announces the district cannot afford raises for the staff that year. He or she recognizes the short and long-term impact of a salary freeze and is sorry to disappoint the staff.

However, he can offer them something every faculty craves: more time. The current school calendar calls for the faculty to return to work from the holiday break on a Friday for a teacher workday. The students will return the following Monday.

As recognition of their efforts, he will waive that workday and allow the teachers to report back the same day as the students.

Not only that, each workday or professional development day on the calendar will be amended to allow the teachers a ninety-minute lunch window with the freedom to leave campus if they like.

Would the teachers prefer a salary increase? Of course.

However, the leader *gets it* and his actions will create loyalty and foster trust, both of which are key factors in a successful workplace culture.

Another example imagines a school district freezing salaries for three or four years in a row and the superintendent not even having the situational awareness to allow the staff to leave campus for lunch when students aren't present.

Sadly, that is not a fictional example. It is a real-life story of a leader being *broken off* from the realities of their employees and failing to treat them like educated professionals.

It reminds me of a meme I saw once: "The beatings will continue until morale improves."

The Seven Strengths Of Leadership

"If your actions inspire others to dream more, learn more, do more and become more, you are a leader."

—John Quincy Adams

As often as leadership fails, one would think the necessary traits would be as elusive as Bigfoot. In reality, the characteristics resemble many of those you would hope to find in a friend or love interest.

Let's start with:

One: Being a great communicator. This doesn't mean they have to have the great oratory skills that helped President Kennedy and Dr. King develop a loyal following, but it certainly helps. Having a dynamic *ability* to communicate is invaluable but fairly rare. As a leader, great communication doesn't have to exist in the form of verbal skills. It can mean having the moxie to know *when* to communicate along with the ability to do so tactfully.

An example: A high school track and field coach has a tough decision to make. The state championships are approaching, and he has five very fast athletes vying for the four positions in the 4x100m relay. Having five athletes capable of competing well in that meet is a luxury most teams never have. The downside is having one athlete who won't compete in the biggest race of the year. The coach is a veteran with strong communication skills. Due to his or her experience, they have metrics in place to measure performance. These are indisputable and the athletes have known what those metrics are the entire season. That reveals a transparency that people appreciate and an evaluation system that will deliver a fair outcome.

But fair isn't always popular.

It is time to talk to the five athletes and announce the four people who will be competing. Rather than putting the fifth runner in an uncomfortable position, the coach pulls them aside privately beforehand.

The coach reminds them of the metrics used, shows the results, and praises the athlete for having a great season. The athlete is reminded that injury or illness to one of the top four runners can still earn them a place in the lineup.

This is a very impressive methodology, but it doesn't prevent the fifth runner from being upset. If that athlete balks or claims it is unfair, the coach can remind them what the decision is based on.

The coach can point back to the beginning of the season when these metrics were explained and, in a supportive tone, remind them that they are traveling with the team with the possibility of competing.

At this point, if the athlete or their parents are still dissatisfied, the coach can ask them one simple question that will allow them to see the situation from the coach's point of view.

The coach might say: "If I give your son or daughter the spot, despite the metrics saying four others are faster, what should I tell the faster athlete and their parents, who is removed from the lineup? They ran faster throughout the season. Ignoring those facts would contradict what I have said all season and put one of the four fastest kids out of the race. How would I explain that to them?"

Because people react differently, this still may not assuage the negative feelings, but the coach has been proactive, supportive, and fair.

The coach also showed compassion to the fifth runner by telling them privately, offered sincere praise, and reminded them that they still may end up competing.

By handling the conflict in this matter, the coach communicated very well and didn't have to be a gifted orator in the process.

Two: Integrity. In the example above, the coach was forthright throughout the entire process. The three runners not involved in the process have goals in play. They appreciate the coach having a system in place, communicating it and putting the fastest team together for the biggest meet.

Let's tweak the example. Let's say the coach knows the family of runner number five very well. They love to go over the chain of command and straight to the superintendent with complaints. They aren't interested in fairness; they just want their child to get what he or she wants.

Knowing this, the coach thinks about runner number four. His family is in shambles and has never contacted district staff or personnel for any reason. An unscrupulous coach could avoid the scathing family by inserting runner number five into the lineup.

Doing so would avoid a clash with the disgruntled parents of runner number five but treat number four poorly by taking advantage of the fact they can only advocate for themselves.

Not only would this be an injustice to runner number four, and a contradiction of the aforementioned evaluative process, but the first three runners would witness the dishonesty, and distrust would take root as they realized the coach isn't interested in being fair.

The coach would have shown no integrity toward his athletes.

Three: Decisiveness. There are times when the need to make a decision falls into the lap of a leader. It may be something so unexpected and potentially awful that it couldn't have been planned for in advance.

A very unfortunate example is all too common in the United States: coming face-to-face with a mass shooter.

Because these awful events are now common, many institutions have regular drills in place to be somewhat prepared.

Harkening back to 1999, the Columbine High School shooting drew the attention of the world. Schools at that time practiced fire drills and in some cases, earthquake and tornado drills.

Intruder drills, which are common today, didn't exist then.

On that tragic day, shots rang out and people were left to their own decisions. In some cases, teachers led their classes to other floors of the building, other rooms, or they stayed where they were.

In the hallways, students running in one direction were passed by students running in the other direction. It was total chaos.

Yet each teacher made decisions. The principals did as well.

In areas like the cafeteria where shootings also took place, students made uninformed, instinctive decisions for themselves and others.

Decisiveness as a leadership trait means several things.

To start, how will a leader respond when confronted with the worst possible circumstances? There are simply times when every head in the room will turn and look at whoever is in charge. The leader must convey confidence and assertiveness with their words and actions.

Another aspect of this is the ability to think ahead and be proactive about as many situations as reasonably possible. That may apply to inclement weather, having a plan in place to shift responsibilities if key staff members miss a meeting, or leave abruptly for another position.

Four: A Charismatic Personality. This trait is similar to the communication trait described previously. Great oratory skills are a gift but are not something everyone can have. Lacking that great speaking ability, a person can still communicate effectively by knowing when to do it and having the tact to do it successfully.

A charismatic personality is a great starting point to build a leader around, but charisma is fairly rare.

Someone with charisma draws other people to them. People instinctively are willing to trust them and their decisions. However, an effective leader doesn't have to have a charismatic personality.

A person that is more low-key but has a quick wit and sense of humor can diffuse many situations. A great conversationalist will be able to explain policies and decisions. People with great personalities are typically kind and approachable. They will have empathy when possible and are typically just easy and pleasant to be around.

Imagine being in a meeting room with other team members minutes before a conference begins.

The boss walks in with a smile, greets everyone, makes a self-deprecating joke about the stain on his or her shirt, followed by humorously recognizing the accomplishments of some people in the room.

Compare them to the stern boss who has never smiled in public. They have no rapport with anyone and don't seem interested in creating a pleasant tone and tenor for the meeting. They are all business and completely lack both personality and charisma.

Said plainly, leaders with personality typically foster successful environments and those with charisma climb corporate ladders more quickly.

In either case, these are the leaders that people choose to work along with or under.

Five: Professionalism. As with many of these traits, professionalism has many variables to it.

Leaders who exude professionalism look the part. They dress like most people aspire to be, even on casual days. They never lead the race to the bottom by abusing "casual day."

They interact with others with appropriate humor and don't fan the flames of inappropriate comments by showing even tacit approval.

Leaders with great professionalism handle tough situations with aplomb. They choose the high road 100 percent of the time. They are also quick to apologize, celebrate the success of others, and choose what's best for the group over trying to be seen as the MVP.

Leaders who reflect this trait are trusted by coworkers to keep confidentiality when appropriate. They don't gossip to one group of workers about anyone else.

Because of all of these strengths, they are trusted as mentors and are always willing to help younger workers gain traction.

Professionalism includes trustworthiness, but is more than that. These are the model employees and problem-solvers.

They are also the employees missed the most when and if they leave.

Six: Definitive Beliefs That Permeate Their Leadership. Let's go way back to the 18th century and a nontraditional English woman named Mary Wollstonecraft (1759–1797). She is recognized for her work titled: *A Vindication of the Rights of Woman* (1792).

Wollstonecraft was well ahead of her time as an intellectual and a writer with the passionate stance that women should be educated as men. Not only did she have progressive thoughts on women's education, but she lived her life in the same manner, taking lovers and having children outside of wedlock.

Though in her day she was considered scandalous, by publishing and living her beliefs, Wollstonecraft strongly influenced writers like Jane Austin, and her writings, particularly her ideas about educating women, became the backbone of the feminist movement.

Seven: Stay Nimble. Sometimes as leaders we don't know what tomorrow will bring or we plan and strategize and the events of time or our market changes, or a new competitor enters. In these cases, we have to be nimble enough to recognize change and to adapt to it.

Susan Wojcicki was a tech visionary with shrewd business acumen at Google. She spearheaded the launch of Google Analytics. When Wojcicki learned about YouTube competing against Google's video service, she orchestrated an acquisition for $1.65B and was named the CEO of YouTube in 2014.

Her priority has been to eliminate policy-violating content, bots, and hoaxes. She credits her leadership success to her flexibility and willingness to adapt to new situations.

About the Author

Kimberly Layne is CEO and Founder of The Kimberly Connection Company (KCC), where she is passionate about turning around the performance of companies by improving "broken cultures" through healthier connections between leaders and their teams.

Kimberly believes that a decade of downsizing, corporate restructuring, process improvement, and automation has taken a toll on front-line workers that has gone unrecognized by company leaders. With the advent of Glassdoor and other public forums for employee grievances, unsettled employees now have a more public and direct impact on a company's growth prospects and they're not afraid to share their opinions publicly.

As a professional speaker, consultant, and leadership advisor, Kimberly speaks to the importance of transparency, vulnerability, and good communication coupled with an organization's need to create a sense of community, and common purpose. She educates, inspires, and coaches leaders at all levels (managers, supervisors, directors, executives) on how to improve culture and build deeper and more sustainable connections.

By working with KCC through proactive mentoring, culture turn-around consulting, and long-term culture maintenance, companies can see significant improvements in employee engagement, quality, innovation and focus that leads to a healthier bottom line. Contact KCC to learn how your leaders can practice "Connected Leadership" for bottom line impact at admin@kimberly-layne.com or visit her website at www.kimberly-layne.com.

Appendix D

Bibliography

1. *2019 NFL Rulebook.* Retrieved from https://operations.
   nfl.com/the-rules/2019-nfl-rulebook/

2. Ackoff, Russell; Addison, Herbert; Bibb, Sally. Management F-Laws: How Organizations Really Work (January 24, 2007)

3. Alexander, B. (2010) The Globilisation of Addiction. Retrieved from: http://brucekalexander.com/articles-speeches/rat-park/148-addiction-the-view-from-rat-park

4. Baron, C. (November 21, 2016). "Number of mobile phone users worldwide from 2015-2020." Retrieved from: https://www.statista.com/statistcs/274774/forecast-of-mobile-phone-users-worldwide

5. Blakemore, E.K. (September 19, 2018). "Five Stories from Trailblazing Women Leaders." Retrieved from: https://www.inc.com/partners-in-leadership/5-stories-from-high-impact-women-leaders.html

6. Blog, unnamed. (August 27, 2015). "How Much Turnover is too much Turnover." Retrieved from: www.vocoli.com/blog/august/how-much-turnover-is-too-much-how-much-too-little

7. Brueck, H. (September 10, 2018). "The US suicide rate has increased 30 percent since 2000 and tripled for young girls. Here's what we can do about it." Retrieved from: https://www.businessinsider.com/us-suicide-rate-increased-since-2000-2018-6/

8. Bort. J. (August 23, 2014). "4 Great Stories About Bill Gates That Show What It Was Really Like to Work with Him." Retrieved from https://www.pjstar.com/article/20140823/BUSINESS/308239994

9. Chivers, J. (November 4, 2009). "What Happens If We Are Not Listened To." Retrieved from: http://EnzineArticles.com/3210708

10. Dr. Erhard-Weiss, D. (November 2018). "Hey, I know you." Retrieved from: https://tinylove.com/us-en/articles/eye-contact-babies/

11. Dunham, R. (March 11, 2017). "Breaking Bread: The Functions of Social Eating." Retrieved from: http//link.springer.com/article/10/1007/s400750-017-0061-4

12. Fehr, J. (August 26, 2019). "The 7 Traits of Truly Horrible Bosses." Retrieved from: https://sba.thehartford.com/managing-employees/horrible-boss-traits/

13. Ferrazzi, K. *Who's Got Your Back*. (New York: Broadway Books, 2019).

14. Griffis, H. (February 27, 2018). Buffer Blog. "State of Remote Work 2018." https://open.buffer.com/state-remote-work-2018/#benefits

15. Howe, D. "Attachment Across the Life Course" (Red Globe Press)

16. Lindberg, S. (September 26, 2018). "What's the difference between hearing and listening?" Retrieved from: https://www.healthline.com/health/hearing-vs-listening

17. Martins, F. (March 14, 2012). "Win the Customer: The Costs of Poor Employee Retention." Retrieved from: http://winthecustomer.com/the-costs-of-poor-employee-retention/

18. Maxwell, C. (May 1, 2014). "Arianna Huffington on how Sleep can Awaken Opportunity." Retrieved from https://www.director.co.uk/9531-arianna-huffington-cover-story/

19. Mineo, Liz. (April 2017). "Good Genes are Nice, but Joy is Better." *The Harvard Gazette*. Retrieved from: https://news.harvard.edu/gazette/story/2017/04/over-nearly-80-years-harvard-study-has-been-showing-how-to-live-a-healthy-and-happy-life/

20. Moreland, J. (May 5, 2013). "The Costs of Ignoring Employee Engagement." Retrieved from: https://www.astcompany.co/3009012/the-costos-of-ignoring-empoloyee-engagement

21. Muhammed, A. (December 21, 2018). "10 Remote work Trends that will Dominate 2019." Retrieved from: https:/www.forbes.com/sites/abdullahimuhammed/2018/12/21/10-remote-work-trends-that-will-dominate-2019/#1a2d1ae77c72

22. Nichols, Michael P. (February 16, 2019). "The Lost Art of Listening: Second Edition. How Learning to Listen Can Improve Relationships." Guilford Publications.

23. O'Donovan, C. (August 20, 2015). "Amazon Rewards Employees Who Stay but Turnover is Still High." Retrieved from: https://www.buzzfeednews.com/article/carolineodonovan/amazon-rewards-employees-who-staybut-turnover-is-still-high

24. Patteni, A. (June 24, 2019). "CDC Report shows Suicide Rates are up 33 percent since 1999." Retrieved from: https://billingsgazette.com/cdc-report-shows-suicide-rates-are-up-since/article_f537e38b-6c5e-5f7a-83f3-f14b610e535d.html

25. Payscale. (2019). Retrieved from: https://www.payscale.com/data-packages/employee-loyalty/full-list

26. Sainato, M. (July 8, 2018). "Amazon has Suppressed all efforts to Unionise." Retrieved from: https://www.theguardian.com/commentisfree/2018/jul/08/amazon-jeff-bezon-unionize-working-conditions

27. Shin, L. (January 31, 2017). "Work from Home In 2017: The Top 100 Companies Offering Remote Jobs." Retrieved from: https://www.forbes.com/sites/laurashin/2017/01/31/

work-from-home-in-2017-the-top-100-companies-offering-remote-jobs/#11a0f96842d8

28. Shoukat, S. (February 4, 2019). "Cell phone addiction and psychological and physiological health in adolescents." *EXCLI Journal*. Retrieved from: https://www.ncbi.nlm.nih.gov/pmc/articles/PMC6449671/

29. Singer, Clifford. (Spring 2019). "Health effects of social isolation and loneliness." *Aging Life Care Journal*. Retrieved from: https://www.aginglifecarejournal.org/health-effects-of-social-isolation-and-loneliness

30. Smith, P. (May 17, 2018). "Working from Home Might Take a Toll on Your Mental Help." Retrieved from: https://www.huffpost.com/entry/working-from-home-mental-health_n_5afd88e2e4b0a59b4e014602

31. "State of Remote Work 2018." Retrieved from: https://open.buffer.com/state-remote-work-2018/#benefits.

32. *The Resourceful Managers Guide to Leadership* (n.d.) Retrieved from https://www.resourcefulmanager.com/guides/successful-leaders/

33. Trapp, R. (May 16, 2015). "Why Successful Leadership Depends on Connection." Retrieved from: https://www.forbes.com/sites/rogertrapp/2015/05/26/why-successful-leadership-depends-on-connections/#167ce09e22ba

34. University of East Anglia. (Secure Base Article) "Attachment Theory." Retrieved from https://www.uea.ac.uk/providingasecurebase/attachment-theory

35. University of Oxford. (March 16, 2017). "Social Eating Connects Communities." Retrieved from: http://www. ox.ac.uk/news/2017-03-16-social-eating-connects-communities

36. Warner, J. (July 10, 2018). "Show me the Money: the ROI on Employee Engagement." Retrieved from: https:// decision-wise.com/show-me-the-money-the-roi-of-employee-engagement/

37. Weiss, R. (September 30, 2015). "The Opposite of Addiction is Connection." Retrieved from: https://www. psychologytoday.com/us/blog/love-and-sex-in-the-digital-age/201509/the-opposite-addition-is-connection

38. World's Greatest Leader of 2019. (n.d.) Retrieved from: https://fortune.com/worlds-greatest-leaders/2019/jordan-peele

39. Young, A. (December 19, 2013). "Amazon.com's Workers Are Low Paid Overworked and Unhappy." Retrieved from: https://www.ibtimes.com/amazoncoms-workers-are-low-paid-overworked-unhappy-new-employee-model-internet-age-1514780

Acknowledgments

A personal note to Gary Dean, for taking the time out of his busy schedule and answering my request to pick his brain regarding "How to build a successful consulting business." Thank you to Suzanne W., a dear and constant friend who always encourages me to go to the next level and inspires me with new ideas (who coincidentally introduced me to Gary Dean). Thank you to all my girlfriends who have seen and heard me cry, throw tantrums, submerge myself in pillows and blankets for days, and who ultimately celebrate with me as I jump for joy at the completion of this book. A special thanks to Erica S., Debra F., Monique D., Candice W., Jill C., and Lori L., and all of the Arras Sisters. All are amazing gifted women I am proud and thankful to call my tribe. These are women who have supported me greatly in this journey to my dreams.

I must also extend a big thank you to Henry DeVries and my family at Indie Books International who created a venue and team of great authors and speakers to provide an abundance of love and support. It is wonderful to be surrounded by individuals that are kind, honest, smart, and givers. Thank you.